HOLDING ON

HOLDING ON

SUNNIE MANN

BLOOMSBURY

First published 1990
Copyright © 1990 by Sunnie Mann

Bloomsbury Publishing Ltd, 2 Soho Square, London wıv 5DE

A CIP catalogue record for this book
is available from the British Library

ısbn 0 7475 0665 5

10 9 8 7 6 5 4 3 2 1

Typeset by Hewer Text Composition Services, Edinburgh
Printed in Great Britain by Butler & Tanner Limited, Frome and London

To my dearest husband, Jackie, in the hope that he will soon be back with me, to read this book.

CONTENTS

ACKNOWLEDGEMENTS

More people than I can name here individually have helped me, not only with this book, but during the difficult months that followed Jackie's kidnapping. I thank every one of them. Above all, I want to acknowledge the help, encouragement and support I have received from Amine Daouk and Brent Sadler, who have unfailingly proved themselves friends indeed. I also wish to thank Mehdi A. Mehdi, not only for his fine photography, but for helping me in so many ways at home in West Beirut, and for escorting me on my journeys from there to Cyprus in the course of the preparation of this book. Anton Gill gave me considerable help with the manuscript and Debby Sadler, Brent's wife, has not only been a good friend, but a recorder of my anecdotes.

I would like to thank all my friends and family in England, including Julie Flint, Susan Barajneh, Christopher Barford and Robert Fisk, for their help and encouragement during the past terrible months; also Mahmoud Khashfi, who has looked after our cars free of charge and proved a real friend.

I would also like to thank Amine Daouk's wife, Kay, and their daughters, Zein, Sarah and Soraya. My neighbours Ingrid Toriz, and Paul and Fadya Arraman and their sons Nadim and Karem, looked after my dog Tara and my cat Sasha during

ACKNOWLEDGEMENTS

my absences in Cyprus. Both in Cyprus and, earlier in Beirut, Hector and Elaine Munro have proved themselves the best of friends.

Last, but not least, I thank my beloved Tara, who has been more than just a pet poodle to me. She has been my constant companion, confidante and friend through all the terrifying and exhausting months of waiting and holding on in West Beirut. Without her love, I wonder if I could have managed. Soon after I finished this book, Tara was forcibly taken from me in the street as we were returning from one of our walks. I am therefore facing the future in even greater loneliness than before.

AUTHOR'S NOTE

Because of the situation in Beirut and the Lebanon, it has occasionally been necessary to change names and disguise certain personalities who appear in the course of this narrative. In some cases, I have left names out altogether. I hope that my readers will bear with me in this, and understand the necessity for it.

1

Jackie's Kidnap

My husband was kidnapped on 12 May 1989.

The day began like any other day. I took Tara, my white toy poodle, for her morning walk, and Jackie tucked into bacon and eggs and wrestled with our French-language newspaper, *L'Orient*. Our one hour of electricity that day fell between noon and one pm. Jackie wanted to get to the bank. The airport had been closed for a long time, so it was difficult to draw cheques on our overseas accounts. He wanted to replenish our dwindling supply of money at the British Bank of the Middle East and then he intended to go to Smith's, in Sadat Street, and stock up with tins of cat and dog food. Smith's was his favourite supermarket. Patrick Smith is half English, half Lebanese, and by some miracle has always been able to keep Jackie furnished with everything he likes to eat, right down to sausages and bacon. I shop there still. The place has been bombed, but it has recovered and goes on trading behind a protective wall of breeze-blocks.

'After I've picked the pet food up, I'll drop into the pub for a pint or two,' he told me.

'OK,' I said. 'But be careful. Look over your shoulder.'

Jackie, who was always very cautious about bombs, never gave a thought to the possibility of being kidnapped. Who would want to kidnap him? he argued. Of what possible bartering value would he be? He wasn't a politician, a journalist, or even a particularly prominent member of the expatriate community. But I had been taken hostage once, and held for several hours. Kidnapping was something I took seriously.

'You and your complex about getting snatched,' he laughed.

'*Malish!*' I said, 'Bye bye', and smiled. He left, and that was the last time I saw him. I can hardly believe that it has already been a year.

I finished all my ordinary morning work, and even managed to do some washing between twelve and one. I had already decided not to go down to the club that afternoon, as there was quite a lot of gunfire in the distance. After lunch I was tired, so I took a siesta.

I must have been more weary than I'd thought, as I didn't wake up until six, to find Tara pawing me. It was time for her walk. I was worried to have slept so long, and got up hurriedly, crossing the room and picking up Tara's lead from a chair. Then I went into the *salon*, as we call the drawing-room in Lebanon, to tell Jackie that I'd woken up and was off. But he wasn't there. I remember thinking that that was odd, because he rarely stayed out late or long, and usually got back in time to hear the news in English on the wireless at 3.15 pm; but I didn't want to believe that anything had happened to him, despite the fear that was already beginning to grow in a corner of my mind, so I told myself that for one reason or another he'd decided to stay on for the afternoon. I took Tara out for her walk.

I returned slowly, willing Jackie to be back; but somehow I knew I would be disappointed. I took my time as I climbed the stairs, putting off the inevitable moment, while Tara kept running on ahead and coming back to see why I wasn't getting a move on.

The emptiness of our flat hit me like a physical blow. It was no good even playing for a few more seconds' illusion and telling myself that he was out on one of the balconies, tending his flowers.

I rang Amine.

'Don't worry,' he said, firmly. 'And don't panic. Just keep calm and leave it to me. There's probably quite a simple explanation. Could he have gone to see anyone after leaving the pub?'

'I can't think who,' I said. 'Nearly all our friends have left town.'

'Pour yourself a beer and have a chat with Tara,' he said. 'I'll do some ringing round for you and then I'll call back.'

Perhaps the longest hour and a half of my life passed before he did so. From the tone of his voice I knew immediately that any feeble flicker of hope I'd kept alive was doomed. 'I've checked all the hospitals and I've rung the pub. Darling, I'm afraid you're going to have to face the fact that he's been kidnapped.' The horror and the loneliness had begun.

The preceding weeks had been harder than most, and just a few days earlier we had been busy simply trying to find food and water. The water supply in West Beirut had long since been cut off, and we were already down to one hour's electricity a day. The Christian leader, General Michel Aoun, had stepped up his bombardment of the Muslim side of the city and we lived in a permanent state of siege. How little we had dreamed of such a situation ever arising when we first arrived in Lebanon forty-five years earlier.

Although there were no stand-pipes near our apartment building in the Raouche district, by the sea in south-west Beirut, we were lucky as far as water was concerned, because not only did the riding club I help to run have its own well, but our dear friend, Amine Daouk, whom I had first met eight years earlier when he brought his daughters to the club, had his own water supply too, as well as his own large private generator – something we could not afford. As often as we could decently impinge on his friendship, and it was safe to drive across town to his place, hot baths and water were freely available.

But petrol was in short supply, and bomb and rocket attacks were frequent and unpredictable. Added to which, the hour's electricity from the main supply was not only erratic, but came at various times of day and night on a rota system that sometimes owed more to theory than practice. Without electricity, the lift in Jaroudy Buildings would not work, and we live on the fifth floor. Carrying twenty-litre cans of water up five flights when you are over seventy, as Jackie is, is no joke. Now, I have to try to manage the job alone. At least I am quite fit. Jackie took no exercise, and he is a heavy smoker. Sometimes he would have to rest for ten minutes on each landing when we were carting water or heavy shopping up to the flat.

Shortly before he disappeared, Jackie planned to set off in his Simca to drive over to Amine's to collect water. At the time, I remember, I was busy catching up on a pile of ironing, before the electricity went off. The telephone rang – it does still frequently work, especially for local calls. It was Jackie's friend Adib, who wanted to know if he was going down to the pub that lunchtime. I was only half listening, but I remember that Jackie told him he'd be too busy that day. Some of the water he was going to collect had already been earmarked for the 'gardens' he maintained on our two balconies. Gardening has always been quite a hobby with him, and he was going to do some repotting and watering that afternoon. Now that he's gone, I try to maintain his plants for him, but I don't have green fingers. At least so far I have managed to keep his three favourite begonias alive.

Jackie told Adib that he would probably see him on Friday – 12 May – at their local, the Captain's Cabin, in Hamra Street. He never got there.

While Jackie went to fetch the water, I finished what ironing I could, and when the electricity went off, I decided, as it was a quiet day, to take my Honda and drive over to the club. Much of the time that I have run or helped with riding clubs in Beirut, they have been located in the district of Bir Hassan. It's a pleasant part of the city, but since the beginning of the war, it hasn't always been a safe one. It is situated between the Palestinian refugee camps of Chatila and Sabra, where the terrible massacres of September 1982 took place as the Christian Phalangists took revenge, under the eyes of the Israeli army of invasion, for the assassination of president-elect Bashir Gemayel. The Sabra camp is only two hundred yards from the club.

The club's fortunes have been chequered, but there has been a nearly continuous membership. That afternoon, I simply wanted to see if anyone had been brave enough to risk the drive out there for a ride. It was different for me; I was professionally concerned, and had the horses to look after. I arrived to find no one there but Abu Assam, the Lebanese instructor whom Amine, who has himself become a keen rider since his daughters started, and now manages the club, had engaged. Abu Assam used to be an army instructor, and ran his own school for a while.

'Did anybody turn up this morning?' I asked.

'No, not a soul.'

'And are we expecting anyone this afternoon?'

He glanced around the empty training ring. 'I don't think anyone will turn up now, frankly.' He meant, and left unsaid, that they would not do so because of the threat of shelling. Sometimes it seems to me that we in Beirut discuss the threat of bombardment and the way it affects our lives the way other people discuss impending rain.

'We'd better exercise the horses.'

By turns we led them out of their boxes, saddled up, and cantered round. We use a right-hand circle – that is to say, a clockwise one – because the Beirut race-course is a right-hand track, and old habits die hard. Of course the race-course has long since been shelled out of existence – it is right by the Museum Crossing of the Green Line; but every racehorse you get in Lebanon, and there are still a few, always starts automatically with the right leg. I remember on that day I rode the little dun mare, Bijou II, because I don't normally like a small horse. They throw me off too easily.

At about five o'clock I decided to pack up, because I wanted to avoid the evening rush-hour (the resilience with which life goes on here is amazing), and also any shelling. The Christians in the East often went in for an evening bombardment. I said goodbye to Abu Assam and got home without more incident than the usual jolting from the pot-holes in the roads and the usual cut-and-thrust of Lebanese traffic. By the time I got back, Tara was impatient for her regular evening walk, something which occasionally seems rather a chore, especially after a day's riding, when the contemplation of our five flights of stairs is daunting. But as Jackie's exercise-taboo extends to walking dogs, I'm the one who has to do it.

I slipped her lead on, shouted hello to Jackie, who was immersed in his gardening, and crossed the broken, dusty road to pass the battered, pock-marked buildings of what had once been one of Beirut's better districts. It is still nearly always safe to let Tara have a run on the beach and, like all her predecessors, she loves to chase the sand-crabs. I like to watch the sunset. I've never tired of it, and it's one of the few things the war hasn't spoilt. There's a legend that if you manage to see the flash of emerald green as the sun touches the sea, you will learn the secret of immortality. I have been looking out for it since 1946, and I still live in hope.

Tara's walk ends at 6.45 pm; like me, she enjoys a regular routine as far as possible. By the time we had tramped up the stairs to the flat it was dusk, and Jackie had abandoned his gardening in favour of preparing dinner while there was still enough daylight to cook by. We cook on butane gas. At the time it was in short supply and we had to ration its use. There was no electric light. We used candles. Over the past few months, I have grown to hate candlelight. Candlelight, and the sight of Jackie's empty chair.

Jackie has always been the cook in our family. In the early days of our marriage, I would offer to perform my wifely duties in that department, but he preferred to do it himself, and he enjoyed it so much that I soon gave up. He loves every aspect of cooking, from the shopping to the preparation to the eating, and one of the best parts of his day is choosing his evening menu from the cookery book. He always has an enormous breakfast, but the one meal he skips is lunch, which he generally takes in the form of the local lager, Almaza. He and his friends meet at the Captain's Cabin nowadays – it's run by an ex-airline pilot and neighbour of ours. They used to go to another place called the Duke of Wellington, but one of the bunch fell out with the landlord, so they boycotted it.

Almaza is too sweet for me; I prefer Amstel. Beer is a great boon out here, especially in the summer, which I've always found unbearably hot. Until recently, I've always spent August in England. It's odd, after so many years, that I've never got used to the heat, and have always disliked it. Jackie is the opposite: he could never move back to England, he says, because the climate would finish him off. As for food, I've always been a light eater. I never feel hungry, and I'm quite happy with fruit and salads; so there was no question of my minding Jackie's monopolising the cooking. He even made the mince pies at Christmas.

I don't like to think about Christmas. Jackie used to be quite boyish about it. He would wrap up all the presents, and no one would be allowed to look at them before the big day. Then there would be just the two of us, and Tara, and Sasha, the Siamese cat. Jackie would bring out all the presents, beautifully wrapped, with ribbons and bows and cards. Then he would start the giving: 'To Tara, from Mummie . . .' And Tara would be given her present and I would undo it for her. There were always dozens of presents, and there would always be ones from our favourite animals of the past: from Gaston, the gazelle we once had, from our little white dog Sealy, and from my favourite dog ever, Husky, who died in 1980, but whose life spanned the transition between the halcyon days in Lebanon and the war years.

I can't remember what Jackie cooked for himself that evening, but it would have been English. He didn't like any other cuisine and he actively disliked Arabic food. In over forty years in Lebanon, he had not learnt a word of French or Arabic, though after our local English-language newspaper, the *Daily Star*, closed down, he got hold of a French dictionary and taught himself enough to get through *L'Orient* every day.

While he was cooking, I went to change my clothes. In early May the heat was still bearable, but Beirut is low-lying and humid, and after the afternoon's riding I was sticky and sandy from the ring. Still, there was no question of a bath – it's not until you're deprived of running water that you learn how much a bath takes, and there was no way of heating that amount anyway. I made do as usual with washing my face, feet and hands.

It was dark by half-past seven. There are few lights in the streets, and little traffic. You would scarcely believe yourself to be in a country town, let alone a capital city, when the war is silent at night in Beirut. We got the candles out, and began the evening ritual of 'Boggle'. 'Boggle' is a word-game played with a number of lettered dice which when shaken in a special box fall into a plastic grid. You have three minutes to make words of more than three letters running in any diagonal or rectilinear line. Jackie, who had long been a crossword buff, invariably won. The candles provide insufficient light to read by, so 'Boggle' was frequently our only diversion in the evenings. Nowadays, if there is no gas and no electricity for light, I stare at the candle and talk to Tara. I cannot describe how interminable the evenings seem.

We played for two hours, and then I went to bed. I was tired after exercising several horses, and I wanted to be asleep before the night bombardment began. If you could not get to sleep first, you would not get to sleep at all; in the silences between the explosions you would lie in the dark, listening for the next barrage. I was lucky that night; I practically slept through the lot, though Jackie stayed up until after midnight. We are very different sleepers. I would always fall asleep immediately, only to wake early to an uneasy kind of half-slumber at two or three in the morning, usually to find Tara pawing my arm. I would drift on until seven or so, and then get up, have an apple and a cup of tea, and take the poodle for her morning walk. Jackie was the opposite: late to bed and late to rise. He would tend to have breakfast around nine, and then return to bed to mull over the papers and the crossword puzzles.

When Tara and I got back, I'd make a stab at the housework. In Beirut the simplest domestic task has become quite a challenge, such as trying to wash all the floors with one cupful of water. As for laundry, I often have to limit myself to looking at the growing pile with equally growing horror. There is a laundry at the bottom of the building, but the washing machines have to be filled by hand, and they have a limitless capacity for water. Once filled, they can be used only when there is electricity. On the whole, our clothes are half-ironed and half-clean most of the time. It is not pleasant.

Jackie's main concern was for the beer supply. 'The most important thing of all is to get down and find some beer,' he'd say. 'We're absolutely out!' In May, the depot we used was closed, and so he'd go off foraging around the various supermarkets that were still operating to see what he could find. I'd stay in the flat until he returned, so that it was never unoccupied.

The whole of one's domestic life is ruled by the clock. It is very irritating. Shopping trips have to be geared to coincide with the time the lift is going to be working, and as there are queues for everything that's in limited supply, tempers are short. If the electricity cuts off while I am still in the lift, I go mad, as I've suffered from severe claustrophobia ever since a bomb trapped me in the basement of a building near Harrods during the Second World War. So far, I've always managed to raise someone within five minutes, but those five minutes can seem like an eternity. And if I have Tara with me, there is an added complication, since by teaching and tradition Muslims have no time for dogs. My rescuer will give me a hand, but refuse to touch Tara. That means fetching a chair and using it to stand on to pull her out myself, since the lift when it sticks invariably does so between two floors.

Now that I have had time to think about things, I wonder for how long we had been living on borrowed time. We were the last English couple living in West Beirut – a dubious privilege in itself – and I am now the last hostage wife there. War, after fifteen years, had become something to which we were used, and I suppose we carried on as if life were normal less from heroism than from a desire to shut out the horrors that surrounded us. Jackie was adamant that we should not leave, and in any case our finances were not sufficiently healthy to allow us anything like the standard of living elsewhere that we enjoyed in Beirut. Our flat is large – it is composed of two adjoining apartments – and we run two cars, but our rent is very low, about £1.50 sterling a month, as we have been there a long time, and once rents are fixed, under Lebanese law they cannot be increased.

The war made its appearance gradually, too, so that it was possible for a long time either to ignore it or to tell oneself that the situation would resolve itself. Against a background of more-or-less peaceful co-existence between the Christians and the Muslims of Lebanon which had continued for centuries, it was easy at first to maintain this delusion.

The ruling people of Lebanon were the Maronite Christians. They had lived here since the sixth century, and took their name from a fifth-century Syrian Christian hermit, St Maro, whose feast day, ironically, is the same as St Valentine's. Until recently, the Maronites also formed the single largest community in the country. Among the Muslims, the Shia outnumber the Sunni. With the influx of Palestinian refugees from Israel and the Gaza Strip to the south of the country in the late sixties, the size of the Muslim population gradually started to increase. Refugee camps set up to receive them became not only effective ghettos but breeding grounds for nationalist militias. Worse, the Palestinians were treated like second-class citizens, and it was the least able and the poorest of them who ended up in the camps. Conditions in the camps were appalling. People lived in extreme squalor, with the barest possible sanitation.

The first clashes between government forces and the guerrillas of the militias occurred as early as 1969. By 1973 these clashes were occurring substantially and regularly, as the Palestinian population of Lebanon had gone up significantly after King Hussein drove them out of Jordan in 1970.

The newcomers added strength to the cause of the oppressed Muslims locally. The rural Shia of South Lebanon were among the poorest in all the country. In playing host to the refugees, Lebanon unwittingly reared a serpent in its bosom. The Christians, rapidly outnumbered, and with a tiny standing army, tried to protect their status as leaders. At the same time, the underprivileged Shias were encouraged to voice their grievances by Kamal Jumblatt, the socialist millionaire who was leader of the Druze sect; though the Druzes are not strictly regarded as Muslims, since their teachings are based on the Bible and Sufi works as well as the Koran. Kamal Jumblatt was also the leader of the Progressive Socialist Party, a position now inherited by his son, Walid.

Lebanon's instability made both its neighbours, Israel and Syria, nervous, and incursions by both in the interests of their own security were inevitable. The Israelis invaded with disastrous results for Lebanon in 1982, although the effect of their invasion was the withdrawal from the country of Yasser Arafat and the core of the PLO. After the death of the strong Christian leader-apparent, Bashir Gemayel, and the revenge massacres at Sabra and Chatila, in effect condoned by Israel, the Israelis themselves withdrew to the south, establishing a buffer zone there. In the north and east of the country, the Syrian army took over. But long before this Beirut had split into the Christian east of the city and the Muslim west. Meanwhile, and especially in the wake of the events of 1982, pro-Iranian and pro-Syrian Islamic groups had established themselves – the Hezbollah and the Amal – and now started to draw each others' blood. Today, the Christians maintain a hold on East Beirut. Syria controls the west of the city, where a Lebanese government attempts to maintain its own existence, in the face of General Aoun, who resides in the basement of the ruined presidential palace at Baabda and refuses to accept its validity. The situation is so volatile that only in mid-November 1989, when I was briefly in Cyprus to discuss the manuscript of this book, the president of only seventeen days, Rene Moawad, was killed by a massive car-bomb in Aishe Bekar Street. Now we have a new president, Elias Hrawi. At the time of writing, he is still alive.

It is against this background, which I have described in a very simplified form, of a violence so intricate in the relationship of its facets that it seems impossible ever to resolve, that we lived, and I continue to live. I love Lebanon, and it is my home, but I would like to leave now, because I am tired. However, I *cannot* leave until I know what has happened to my husband. The waiting is the biggest hell of all.

2

WARTIME

How little we know of the direction in which our lives will take us. I was born in Weston-super-Mare in Somerset. My father was the director of a large coal business, and that meant that we led a fairly nomadic existence for several years; but when I was thirteen we settled in Ludlow, in Shropshire. My parents sent me to a private school there and then, shortly afterwards, to Cheltenham Ladies' College – which I hated. True, it was a great place for sport; but the sport they liked and the sport I liked were quite different. My love of horses had begun with my first ride at the age of three, in a basket attached to a Shetland pony; but my older brother Glyn never showed the slightest interest in matters equestrian, and neither had either of my parents, so I don't know where I got it from. It has been my life, though; apart from the war years in England, I've always ridden.

At Cheltenham, however, they were all hockey-mad, and if you didn't play, you just weren't accepted. I do remember that I somehow got into the Third Eleven once. I am quite small, and in those days I was tiny. My most vivid memory of the day of my first match, and indeed practically my only recollection of Cheltenham, was being out on the field in the cold. Suddenly, from nowhere, the ball landed at my feet and I looked up to see a squad of enormous girls from the other side bearing down on me, wielding their sticks in what seemed to me to be a most ferocious manner. I didn't think. I just turned and ran. Of course, I was kicked out of the Third Eleven and never invited to play for it again.

School was not a place where I flourished. There were only two subjects that I really took to, History and English; I was a complete flop at Science and Mathematics, and because I hated hockey I didn't make any real friends. There was one girl called Kay, whom I shared a room with for a short time. At Cheltenham in those days we boarded in rooms of only two or three beds. Kay was very handsome in a mannish sort of way that was accentuated by her short, severe haircut. Unfortunately we had not been sharing long before she decided that she was in love with me. It was my first experience of lesbianism and I didn't like it; I had just discovered sex myself and I knew perfectly well that I wasn't keen on girls in that way. We had a dreadful row, and they moved us to different rooms.

The reason school was an unhappy time for me was partly my own fault. My brother had always given me a rough time at home, and although I adored him, he always rejected me. I think part of the problem was that he had been a beautiful baby and toddler, and the apple of everyone's eye. Then, after three years, I came along. I wasn't by any means even a pretty child. In fact I was rather plain, with a red face and an ugly topknot of black hair. But I was the new baby, and I don't think Glyn ever forgave me for superseding him as the centre of attention. I remember that for my fifth birthday my Aunt Gladys, of whom I was very fond, gave me a little enamelled pendant in the shape of a heart. I was terribly pleased with it and took it to Glyn to show him. I found him in the nursery and stood in the doorway with the pendant in my outstretched hand. I think he meant just to slam the door in my face, but it caught my hand, and he'd swung it with such force that he broke my finger. I was in hospital for about a week. Glyn was not at all remorseful. We didn't actually become friends until adulthood, and then largely because while he'd been in the RNVR he'd married a Wren, and she and I got on very well indeed, Glyn became a bank manager after the war, and now he's retired he lives in Penarth, near Cardiff. All the family seem to have ended up there: my nephew David and his wife, and my own daughter Jennifer.

As for my parents, they never got on very well together either, so we were a family that lived together only in the sense of all being under one roof. I think my parents were chalk-and-cheese. Father was full of life and sparkle. My mother, who had been a schoolteacher before she married, came from a rather narrow Welsh background. The way things turned out, I always took my father's side and Glyn my mother's.

The great redemption of youth was riding. All through my childhood and right through my teens I rode whenever I could, joining the local club wherever we were. Apart from the Shetland pony, the first horse I remember was called Jack, who belonged to a local farmer. I'd probably be a bit snooty about his quality now, but at the age of six or seven I thought he was a god.

After I had left Cheltenham, rising sixteen, the family wanted me to go back to Ludlow and become a 'young lady', but that did not appeal to me at all. I found Ludlow claustrophobic, and because of an early affair of the heart, I was eager to escape from it; so I started answering advertisements in the London papers to see if I could find a job as a nanny. Anything, I thought, to get me to London. My parents, who had ambitions of quite another sort for me, were not pleased; but I have always been stubborn, and even defiant, and I had to get away from Ludlow.

I found a job as companion to a girl called Susan, who was only two years younger than me, and lived in Lancaster Gate, where her father was a doctor. This was my first real taste of London, and I loved it. Part of my job was to accompany Susan to the theatre, and to musuems, concerts and exhibitions. As I was also given a generous amount of time off, I had a whale of a time. I got to know most of the night-clubs and restaurants that were fashionable then. The knowledge that I built up was to be very useful to me in the near future – nearer, certainly, than I dreamt then. But before war broke out, my life was to take one or two more twists and turns.

After two very happy years with Susan's family, I gave in to family pressure and returned to Ludlow. I still don't know why: perhaps absence had made the heart grow fonder; perhaps I wanted to prove to myself one way or the other that the romantic reason for leaving in the first place was well and truly over and done with. Little did I know that romance – or, more accurately, marriage – was soon to threaten from quite another quarter.

I'd known John ever since I was a little girl, as he was one of my father's closest friends. I probably regarded him as a sort of *ersatz* uncle. John, it appeared, had always had quite a soft spot for me, and now that I had returned from London no longer a little girl but very definitely a young woman, he decided that I would do for him. That's almost certainly how it happened. I'm less sure about my own reasons for rushing into matrimony at the age of seventeen with a man twenty-two years my senior; I can only think that the main attraction was the chance of escape from my not very happy family life. I also urgently wanted to love and be loved. Perhaps I mistook the desire for the thing itself. As for John, he wanted me as a kind of table-dressing, icing on the cake, an adornment rather like a glorified button hole. He was never a lover, and we had nothing in common. He didn't hunt, so there was no horse-connection; though that was in his favour. I could never have married anyone who went in for fox- or stag-hunting; I'm too fond of animals.

John's sports were fishing and shooting – and golf. I'll come back to golf in a moment. In the meantime, as preparations for the marriage went ahead, I was slightly bemused by my parents' enthusiasm. Looking back, I can understand it better than I used to. My father saw his unruly daughter marrying his best friend – an older man who would be able to keep her under control. Added to which, John was not only the second heir to a title – he was always saying, 'When Derek dies, you will be *Lady*

So-and-So' – but very rich indeed. None of that interested me, and although money's nice, I couldn't care less about titles.

For our honeymoon we went for a cruise on a liner. John thought I would enjoy that, and I did, though, as a plaything, I was never consulted about what I would like to do myself. Even so, I had a ball on the ship. I was for ever playing deck tennis and quoits, and in the evenings there was always dancing. John used to sit placidly and watch. Occasionally I would go over to him and try to be wifely:

'Don't you want to dance, darling?'

'No, no – you enjoy yourself,' he'd say. And my God, I did! But I wasn't far into married life before I realised that I'd gone down a cul-de-sac. I wanted to live life for myself, especially at that age, and I wanted love, and my own experiences. All I got was a pat on the head.

We had not been back from our honeymoon long before I discovered that I was pregnant. I wasn't pleased. I thought I was far too young – irresponsible even – to have a child. But it was too late for regrets by then, and in any case, there would have been little I could have done to prevent it. When the time came, I went through three days of dry labour – the pain nearly killed me. Jennifer was born eventually, but from that minute on I never wanted to see another child, or John's face, again. I wanted to escape, and never ever more to hear the word 'marriage'. Overnight I changed from a happy-go-lucky teenager into a nervous wreck. The disaster was compounded by the physical complications which set in after the birth. I was in such a state that they had to perform a pan-hysterectomy on me; they took everything out except my ovaries. I could never have another child.

We tried to patch up our marriage for our daughter's sake. We moved to Hayling Island, near Portsmouth, and for a time there was a lull. But John was a very keen golfer, a Plus One, or something – whatever they are called. I, of course, wanted to ride; but that didn't fit into John's scheme of things. 'Why don't you take up golf, dear?' he would suggest, and he persisted.

He said he'd take me up to Lillywhite's and see me fully kitted out – 'And then you can take lessons from the Pro.' I thought, anything for a peaceful life, and so off we went, and I was dressed from top to toe in the best golfing outfit money could buy – after which a pleasant young gentleman dug out the best kit, to go with it. I had the right trousers, the right jacket, everything, right down to the little things you stick in the ground to put your ball on. A full set of clubs. I even had a little peaked cap. I shudder to think how much it all cost, but it didn't raise a glimmer of enthusiasm in me.

Back at Hayling Island, I embarked upon my course of lessons. After three, it was clear that I wasn't ever going to shine as a golfer. 'Mrs Wilson, can't you concentrate a little more?' the Pro kept imploring. 'Can't you keep your eye on the ball, and swing your right arm up and hit it?' Nothing doing. I couldn't hit the bloody thing. If he'd poured ten gins down me I still couldn't have hit it! But John was not deterred. One morning, the inevitable happened.

'Now darling, you've had plenty of lessons, so I think we should go round the course together.'

'Should we?' I replied timorously.

'Yes, dear. I'll help you.'

In other departments the attempt to shore up the marriage had not been successful, so there was already a lot of tension between us. Golf for me proved the last straw. Surely John could see that it wasn't a game I was ever going to take to, or enjoy.

We started off, but after only two holes I got into a thing called a bunker, which is a kind of sandpit designed as a deliberate obstacle. This one was quite high. I remember that it was a nice day and the sea – the golf course at Hayling is right by it – looked lovely. But there I was in the bunker.

'Now darling,' said John, 'Take your mashy [or whatever it was called] and chip it out.'

I tried.

'Chip it out!' said John, with more edge in his voice.

'How? It's all sand!'

'You really must concentrate. You must keep your eye on the ball and swing your club.'

I swung about ten times, and all that happened was that I became covered in sand. I also became hysterical. I bent down and picked up the obstinate ball and its tee. Taking my golf bag in my other hand, I walked the short distance to the rail separating the edge of the golf course from the sea. I took off my little peaked cap and threw it over. By this time John had caught up with me.

'What are you doing, darling?' he said.

I said, 'I'm dropping the bloody golf-clubs into the sea.' And I did.

Then he lost his temper. 'How dare you?' he shouted. 'Do you know how much all that cost me? What are you doing?'

I said, 'My jacket's going now.' He was screaming at me. I said, 'If you say one more word, I'll take off my trousers and they'll go in too.'

He walked away. A couple of months later we filed for divorce, and that was the end of my first marriage. It had lasted about three years. In the meantime, war was looming, so I took Jennifer to Ludlow, to live with my mother. Then I went back to London.

I had been accepted as a volunteer driver for the St John Ambulance Brigade. While John and I were breaking up, Hitler had invaded Poland, and we were now at war. Looking back on those days, I remember first all the fun we had, not the horror which went with it, though that aspect is not possible to forget. The air raids were dreadful. Driving to bombed buildings, we would rescue whoever we could, working among the smoking ruins and the scattered limbs of the wounded and the dead, loading the maimed on to the ambulances as the bombs continued to fall. The worst bombs of all were those which the Germans let fall on parachutes. You would stand there and watch them gradually sailing down, and think, my

God, is it going to come down there, or there? The minute you started to move, the wind would veer round and blow the bomb after you. 'Christ, it's coming down over here! Down on the ground, everyone! Hands over your heads!' Then the bomb would fall a little distance away after all. And you'd laugh with relief and say, 'Thank God,' and love life.

But for all that, I have been far more frightened of the bombs and shells in Beirut than I ever was during the Blitz or any of the other raids on London. It was worst of all during the Israeli invasion in 1982, because then the bombardment was so fast and so concentrated. In London fifty years ago, you heard the planes coming, and the sound of the air-raid sirens, so you had time to prepare yourself, or run to a shelter. But in Lebanon distances are small and jets are so fast that they were on you almost at the same moment that you heard them. One minute they'd be a dot in the sky, the next, screaming overhead; and there was no warning at all.

Another element that makes Beirut now more frightening than London then is the quality of the buildings. Most of the blocks in Beirut were run up quickly and cheaply when the town was booming: none of them has the solidity that most buildings in London have, and they collapse easily and completely when hit, so that many people die trapped under the rubble. The other thing that London had, and Beirut hasn't, was efficient fire services, even when things were at their worst. During the Blitz, the fire brigade was marvellous – they always arrived in no time at all. In Beirut, they would arrive, but then run out of water, so they'd have to drive down to the sea to try to refill their tank, and meanwhile, you could be frying.

The one thing that is the same in Beirut as it was in London is the need to keep your sense of humour. Without it, you'd be finished. I remember the parties we used to have in the Underground. They were splendid, but as everybody used to make for the Tube in the evenings it was a case of first come, first served, if you wanted a space to sleep for the night. There'd be fish and chips, and people playing records of Vera

Lynn, or organising impromptu concerts of their own. Like a kind of merry hell, with the noise and the awful smell of chips, and the trains rumbling through until midnight. Everyone was always drunk down there – you couldn't cope otherwise.

There are other elements which make life in Beirut today harder than it was in London then. The most obvious is the lack of camaraderie. When the fighting is at its height, everyone who can leaves the city. They leave the country altogether, or they get out to the countryside or to the hills, away from the war. They rent skiing chalets at Ferayah, for example. During the whole of the summer of 1989, immediately following Jackie's kidnapping, I was alone – my district was virtually deserted. Then there are the car-bombs. They are worse than the raids, because at least you can see a raid. A car-bomb can be concealed in any street, at any time. If you thought about it too much, you'd never go out at all.

Perhaps the worst thing is the mistrust. I have got to the point where I barely say anything to any stranger in case they are either spies for the Hezbollah or members of Syrian Security. One can treat the most innocent remark with suspicion. If someone asks you what you were doing yesterday, you might well snap back: What's that got to do with you? You are on your guard all the time, thinking that people are trying to find out what you are thinking. And you ask yourself if you might have offended anyone dangerous – an Amal militiaman at a checkpoint? A Syrian soldier? I know that I am followed, and that my phone is tapped, by Syrian Security. I don't know who it is that periodically telephones in the middle of the night and suggests it would be better if I left Beirut.

Driving ambulances in the London air-raids was an extraordinary experience. We were never regularly teamed up with the same orderlies – we'd just get a telephone call and be asked to report for duty. I'd put my little cap on my head and pin on my badge. I had no medical experience at all, but I was a good driver, and that's what they wanted. It wasn't always enough.

Real ambulance drivers have to pass exams, and train in basic mechanics; but during the war, the ambulance brigades were glad just to get people who were prepared to drive under fire – they didn't mind if you couldn't change a tyre, or knew nothing about oil levels. I remember one puncture we had quite near where I lived in Chelsea. My orderly was a cockney who at least had had a bit of medical training, but I don't know if he was any more mechanically minded than me.

'We've got a puncture,' he said.

'Yes,' I said.

'Well, you're the driver, you'll have to change the tyre,' he told me.

I looked at him, 'Um, yes, I suppose I will.' But I went on sitting there. I hadn't a clue what to do.

'Look, love,' he said. 'There's bombs falling. Get on with it.'

I stared at him. 'I don't know how to.'

'Blimey! Bloody society woman, driving goddam ambulances and can't even change a bleeding wheel!'

'Yes,' I said. 'I'm very sorry; but I can't change a wheel. I simply don't know how.' I couldn't blame him for being angry. I couldn't even blame him for calling me a society woman. That's what I was, in those days. Despite the war, London was at my feet.

My ambulance career came to an abrupt end when I got a bit of shrapnel in my arm. We were out on our usual safari – in fact I was with the same cockney orderly that night. A bomb hit just in front of us, making a big crater, and the ambulance objected. Like a horse, it stood up on its hind legs. I was thrown out and fell on to the shrapnel. It slit my arm as neatly as a butcher's knife, and made a nasty wound. Nothing dramatic, but very painful. My cockney escaped unhurt, and flagged down another ambulance which was passing. Ours was a wreck.

'My driver's buggered,' he shouted to the other ambulance. 'We've got to get her to a hospital.'

I spent about ten days getting patched up; then my father came to collect me, and carted me off to convalesce in Ludlow.

During my ambulance driving days I had plenty of opportunity to look up some of the haunts I'd discovered during my first stay in London. I'd become very friendly with several of the actors who worked at the Royal Court Theatre, since we frequented the same pub, the Antelope, which was just round the corner in Eaton Terrace. London was an exciting place for attractive girls then, and quite innocently you got to know lots of interesting people if you made half an effort. At the Antelope we'd drink, and chat across the bar, and if there was a raid we'd all dash for the shelter together. To pass the time away, everyone would tell their life story. People made friends quickly. There were none of the restraints of peacetime.

Among the actors I got to know were Basil Radford and Basil Rathbone. Basil Rathbone was already a big star, and when he went off to entertain the troops he let me live in his house in Cliveden Place – a stone's throw from the Antelope – as his guest. It was about that time that I met my second husband at a cocktail party. We still had them, in the midst of the war and in the thick of the bombing. He was a major in the Royal Marines, very attractive, and his name was Keith McWhirter. We married after three days. Not long afterwards, he left to rejoin his regiment, and two months later I heard that he had been killed in action. Where, I never discovered. I hardly knew him, never met his parents. I am sorry to say that his death didn't mean a great deal to me. An emotional rip-tide runs in wartime. Everyone was either sleeping together or rushing off to get married within days. If he'd lived, we probably wouldn't have stayed married. Our love affair wasn't real. In those days you thought every night could well be your last, and you lived accordingly. I was twenty years old.

I had made great friends with a nursing auxiliary called Paddy Naismith, and we remained close until Jackie and I left for Cyprus in 1945. Paddy was a redhead, and one of the most dynamic people I have ever met. She was lovely, life filled her up; and she was also very promiscuous. She'd go to bed with anyone who attracted her. Canadian, American, Australian, British – anyone who was on leave in London and needed a rest from the war was made welcome by Paddy. We both worked very hard, but Paddy always found time and the energy for sex. I learnt most of my bad habits from her, but I am sorry to have lost touch; the last I heard was that her brother Dermot, who was a good friend, had been killed in action.

Apart from the Antelope, one of our most important meeting places was the Brevet Club in Charles Street. It was bombed out in the course of the war, but in its day it was the place where all the fliers went. It wasn't a cabaret club; it just had a bar and a good restaurant, but all the Allied airmen in London used it. It was here, in the course of a casual conversation, that Paddy and I learnt of the plastic surgery unit at East Grinstead hospital. Many fighter pilots and bomber crews sustained severe burns in action, and at East Grinstead one of the great pioneer plastic surgeons, Archie McIndoe, was engaged in rebuilding their faces and bodies. The process was a painful one, and could take years.

Paddy thought it would be a good idea if we could organise some kind of unofficial rehabilitation programme for those men who had been through the main surgery and were now out-patients. We made a few enquiries, and visited the hospital, where our suggestions were welcomed. Some of the men had been very badly deformed, but that did not deter us. If anything, it had the opposite effect. I remember one poor boy called Paul. He'd been the rear gunner in a Lancaster bomber, and found himself trapped in his turret when the plane was hit and caught fire. McIndoe built him a whole new face – his nose had been burnt off, his eyelids, everything.

Through a director of the building company, McAlpine, Paddy managed to borrow a flat next door to the Dorchester Hotel for the boys to stay in when they came up to town for the nights out we arranged for them. Both of us had quite an 'in' at the Dorchester at the time, and the staff were more than cooperative. Robert Morley was often around, too, and he chipped in with help and champagne. We were able to arrange monthly parties, held at the house, with drinks, dinner and dancing. We rustled up all our prettiest girlfriends as partners.

This was in 1941, and plastic surgery was in its infancy. The boys loved the parties, but they had no illusions about what they looked like. They were very brave, and everyone was marvellous to them. Or almost everyone.

On one occasion we were entertaining six or seven fliers at the Dorchester as usual. We had barely started the first course when the Maître d'Hôtel, whom I knew very well, came over to our table looking embarrassed.

'What's the matter?' I asked.

He was discreet. 'I'm terribly sorry, Mrs McWhirter,' he said, 'but I've had a complaint from the two couples dining together over there.' He hesitated. 'I wouldn't bother you normally, but as they are very old, regular customers of ours . . . we don't really want to offend them.'

'What's the complaint?' I asked, genuinely puzzled. We had been behaving, I thought, in an exemplary fashion. Everyone was correctly dressed, and there hadn't even been a raucous laugh.

The Maître D cleared his throat nervously. 'They feel that – um – it's not quite the proper thing to bring men in here who look so dreadful. That's what they said.'

I could hardly believe my ears. 'They said *what*?'

'I'm very sorry. It's nothing to do with me. You know how we love to have you here.'

'Take me over to them,' I said.

Even today I boil with anger when I think about this episode. I am surprised that I managed to have so much self-control then. When I arrived at their table, I said, 'I gather you have made a complaint about the appearance of my guests.'

One of the women spoke for the group. 'We certainly have,' she said. 'It's upsetting our dinner.'

'Madam,' I said, 'I'm going to upset you even more now. Do you know why those boys look like that? Because they've been defending you in the Battle of Britain – so that you can sit on your fat *derrières* and eat your food in the Dorchester Hotel; and yet you dare to criticise them! This is what I think about you and your complaint, madam.' I was holding a large glass of gin and tonic and I tipped it over her head.

They left, and we never had any more trouble. We never saw them again, in fact.

I returned to my table. Among the young men up from East Grinstead that day was a twenty-six-year-old Sergeant Pilot called Jack Mann.

3

ROMANCE AND MARRIAGE

Our romance didn't start immediately. It began the following New Year's Eve, when we were dancing together at the
Dorchester to a tune called 'Yours'. We got terribly sentimental.
I don't think that feeling has ever quite gone away. We still love
each other. I wouldn't say that we are 'in love' now, but I know
that Jackie would do anything for me, in any emergency, and
I hope I'm doing everything I can for him in his emergency. I
wouldn't want anybody else, though I can safely say that we
have had the most difficult of marriages during the past fifteen
years in Lebanon. The years preceding the war were very easy,
by contrast, because we were having a wonderful time, enjoying
everything, doing things together. Since the troubles came, it
hasn't been so simple. We have arguments about who will go
down in the lift to get the shopping, or who will carry the
water up the stairs. I am sad that lately Jackie has aged. Since
the pub he ran, which I will describe later, was blown up, he
has made less and less effort. Certainly the stress of living in
Beirut makes one listless, especially if one has few interests;
and Jackie will rarely go out, other than in the course of his
narrow routine.

But we still love each other. And occasionally, when we
hear 'Yours' on the wireless or the television, we remember

that New Year's Eve forty-seven years ago, and we both get terribly sentimental all over again. At the time, it was a hit. Everyone was singing it. The Dorchester always played it:

> Yours till the stars lose their glory,
> Yours till the birds fail to sing.
> Yours till the end of life's story,
> This pledge to you dear I bring;
> Yours to the end of a lifetime . . .

We had it as our wedding march too. It's always been our song.

Jackie's new skin has blended in with the old over the fifty-odd years that have passed since his Spitfire landed in flames in a field in Kent. He has always sported an RAF moustache, and for the past ten years he has worn Victorian side-whiskers too; between them they disguise any great irregularity on his face. His legs, however, are still badly scarred, and even after all this time they give him pain, especially in hot weather. I sometimes wonder if the disfigurement of his legs isn't one of the reasons why he has never taken up swimming again, despite living in Lebanon. When we first arrived in Beirut, I took up water-skiing. I loved it, and tried to persuade him to have a go, but he never would.

By the time I met him he was an out-patient at East Grinstead. Between operations, he was able to travel up to London, and when petrol permitted he would use his lovely little open-top MG – a proper sports car, with a square radiator and wire wheels. For some reason, we christened her 'Susan', and she was the first of three to bear the same name.

His mother and father, Frederick and Edith, lived just outside Northampton in a village called Bramley, where they ran a delightful pub called the Windmill. I took to them immediately – they were the warmhearted family I had been looking for all my life. Jackie's sisters, Betty and Madge, and I got on like a house on fire from the word 'go'. While we were courting,

Jackie and I used to go up there to stay whenever we had a free weekend, I was especially fond of his mother, whom I gave the nickname Mop, for her mass of thick grey hair. She was the only one of my three mothers-in-law I can honestly say I liked. I detested the first, and of course I never knew the second.

As a Spitfire pilot, Jackie had seen a good deal of action, and had been awarded the DFM. He had been shot down six times, but always managed to get his plane back to England, preferring the risk of a crash-landing to life in a prison camp, for reasons which I will explain. Mop used to tell a story about the events which followed one of his crashes. The family received notification from the Air Ministry that Jackie had been killed. They could collect his body from the mortuary at Petersfield. Mop, Madge and Betty hired a hearse, and mournfully set off to fetch him. When they arrived, they sought out the Flight Lieutenant who was in charge of the mortuary. He went through his own list, but couldn't find Jackie's name on it. He went off to double-check, but soon returned, smiling.

'Mrs Mann,' he said to Mop. 'I think there must have been a mistake; one which will make you happy, but someone else very sad.' It turned out that there was another pilot called Mann on the lists of those killed: his name and Jackie's had been confused, and the two men's families were sent the wrong telegrams. Jackie was in hospital, not well, but alive, and out of danger. Mop and the girls drove back to Bramley with the hearse covered in flowers, and stopped at every pub on the way to celebrate. Though obviously a tragic story for the dead pilot's family, Mop would tell it because of its funny-happy side for her, and during the war we used to look for every flicker of hope.

Jackie was educated at the local grammar school in Northampton, and perhaps surprisingly in view of how he was later, he was very good at sport. After school he went to France with a friend for a while in order to learn French, but he never managed to, and since then he has been adamant about not going there to live, which from my point of view is a pity, because I love it. Returning to England, he joined the RAF Reserve, which meant that he was already qualified as a pilot when war broke out. He was called up immediately, and went straight on to Spitfires. Planes to him were like horses to me – he had an instinctive feeling for them, and could fly anything after only a short time at the controls.

Sometimes I wonder how it was that we got married, because Jackie hated horses then, and never showed any interest in them afterwards. For myself, I had never been in a plane, so I didn't know if I would like them or not. What I did like, and took to immediately, was the atmosphere of the RAF. The tension of facing death every day bred a devil-may-care attitude. There was no sentimentality at all: if you went, you went. It was a risk all the Spitfire and Hurricane pilots took, and had to take. More died than came back, but the ones that did come back were heroes. I used to like to go out to look at the fighters drawn up on the airfield. Each plane – Jackie's included – had 'notches' painted on it to mark the number of 'kills' it had made – and there was always a brisk rivalry over who had the most.

Each time he was shot up, Jackie had done his damndest to get back, not just because training a pilot was a long and expensive business, but because he had a horror of being taken prisoner and confined. It is that knowledge which makes me so fearful for him now that he is a hostage.

I met him when he was recovering from the effects of his last crash. A shell had hit the petrol tank of the Spitfire just as he was starting to cross the Channel from the Continent. He told me later that it had crossed his mind at the time to take the safer option, turn back, and try to bring the plane down somewhere on the mainland; but then his phobia about being taken prisoner overwhelmed him, and he steered out to sea. He said that he would rather take his chance of dying in the Spitfire than face the certainty of years in a POW camp. He just made the British coast, and managed to land in a field before the petrol tank went up. He says now that the shock and the pain together were so great that he felt nothing during the seconds that he was struggling free of the cockpit. He got caught in the parachute harness at first, and lost precious moments. Eventually he managed to kick free, but by then his legs were on fire. He fell out of the plane, and managed to stand up and stagger away. Then, of all things, he remembered that he had a camera in his pocket, took it out, focussed on the burning wreck, and took some pictures. Immediately after that the pain hit him, and he collapsed.

Farmers working in a neighbouring field had seen him come down. They carried him to the farmhouse and phoned for an ambulance. All the newspapers carried the story – the fact that he'd taken those photographs was considered remarkable. But that was not the only crash in which he was injured. On another occasion he got a bullet through the seat of his cockpit which went straight into his *derrière*. He's got an enormous scar there. That, he says, was not a pleasant experience, but everything else he just laughs off. He is not one to talk about himself.

At East Grinstead, they had to do a lot of work on him. He was blind for six days, and they weren't sure at first if he would recover his sight. They had to reconstruct his cheekbones and the entire area around his eyes. Luckily, his helmet had saved his forehead and skull, and his microphone/oxygen mask had protected most of his nose, mouth and chin. Even so, the series of skin grafts he underwent was gruelling. They took the replacement skin for the face from undamaged parts of his thighs; half the time he would be attached from the face to the thigh by a roll of skin, until it could be smoothed in. That arrangement was unimaginably painful, and not very easy to look at. But we both idolised Archie McIndoe, and had complete faith in him. Altogether, three-quarters of Jackie's face had to be remade.

But he never had a chance to feel embarrassed about his looks, once he'd met me. He came to the Dorchester frequently, and I would just take him and whirl him round the dance floor. I thought he was romantic and dazzling, and I must have made some impression on him, too, because it wasn't long before he was talking marriage. He was all for it, and as soon as possible; but I had become a little shy of that institution. Still, after we'd seen each other four or five times, we decided to try living together at least – I still had the use of Basil Rathbone's house in Cliveden Place, where I was living alone with my Pekinese dog, Waffle.

We were joined there by Jackie's beautiful young Alsatian bitch, Vixen. Vixen was very fond of me, and not at all jealous, Alas, that was not to be our experience with one of Jackie's later dogs, in Lebanon!

Eventually, he had recovered sufficiently to return to flying, though he was not to see active service again.

He was sent to Croydon Airport to undertake delivery flights. This might entail, for example, flying a Wellington up to Norfolk, and bringing a Spitfire back. Because of his facility with planes of all kinds, Jackie was particularly good at this type of work. We were able to find a house in Purley, which acquaintances let us have free in return for 'house-sitting' for them. It was fun there. By this time my ambulance-driving days were behind me, and we would always have a houseful of friends. Everyone lived together in those days.

Best of all was Vixen. She'd go to the airport with Jackie in the mornings and wait for him in the control tower all day. Astonishingly, no matter what kind of aeroplane he came back in, she'd know it was him flying it, and she'd be off across the runway to meet him, sometimes jumping on to the wing as he taxi'd in. Croydon was a busy airport, and the control tower used to have to transmit a warning: Dog on the runway.

One of our dearest friends, with whom we are still in touch, was Jackie's old Squadron Leader, 'Wally' Wallens. As soon as it was clear how serious Jackie was about me, Wally started putting pressure on him to get a commission. Jackie had always fought shy of this, because, he argued, you had twice the fun and half the responsibility when you were 'other ranks'. Wally was a real character – quite small and, like many small people, a bit bombastic, but a brilliant pilot despite the fact that he had also sustained grim leg injuries, and walked with a pronounced limp. Jackie let Wally persuade him to sit the examination required to become a Pilot Officer, passed, and took his commission.

Then Wally turned to me and said, 'Right, the next item on the agenda is that you two get married.'

I dithered for a couple of weeks, but eventually I gave in and the chaps at Croydon set about arranging our wedding. I know that Wally was behind the main present: only he could have thought it up.

We were married on 18 June 1943, a week after Jackie's birthday, at Croydon Register Office. When we came out, the other pilots formed an arch of propellor blades for us – eight on each side – as was the custom. Then came the first surprise: waiting to take us to the reception at the RAF mess was a beautiful horse and carriage, decorated with red, white and blue flowers.

At the reception, which was enormous, everyone got splendidly tight, hoping to God that they would not have to fly that evening. Then the Croydon wedding present was produced. It was a large, oblong box, not unlike a small coffin.

'What on earth is that?' I said.

They grinned and said, 'Open it and see!'

Jackie was given a large screwdriver and with it managed to prise the top off. Inside were five hundred brand-new bronze threepenny-bits, which the men had been collecting ever since our wedding was announced. On top of them lay a splendid silver salver engraved with the names of all the crews at Croydon who'd ever flown with Jackie. We had a perfect day, and luckily no one had to fly that night. Later, it took us hours to count out all the threepenny-bits, and get them to the bank. It was a typical Wallens joke. But it was a wonderful wedding – the best of the three I've had.

By enormous luck, we were able to take ten days' leave for our honeymoon. One of the other nice wedding presents we had was a collection of petrol coupons. Everybody had clubbed together to give us their share so that we could take 'Susan I' down to Cornwall. There wasn't room in the MG for us, our luggage and Vixen, so she had to stay with Wally; but Waffle was small enough to squeeze in and keep us company. The war had barely touched Cornwall, and for a short time that summer we were able to enjoy an illusion of peace. In fact, the drive down from London was so pleasant that it suggested the idea for another, much longer drive in 'Susan III' which we undertook almost exactly six years later.

We managed to spend the rest of 1943 together, but at the beginning of the following year Jackie's skill caused him to be transferred to transatlantic supply flights. He would be based in Montreal, and for the next eighteen months or so we would see each other only once or twice a month. But the Montreal posting wasn't all bad. Jackie loved Canada, and made many new friends there. From our point of view, every time he came home was like Christmas, for Canada was not subject to the same stringent rationing that we had. We were getting two ounces of butter a week, for example, and one egg. The egg was regarded as a great treat, and long, serious discussions would go on about how it would be eaten to elicit the greatest pleasure. I remember the Boiled, Scrambled and Fried schools of thought. Into this dearth Jackie would bring nylons, chocolate, coffee, oranges, booze, shoes – all unheard of luxuries. My daughter Jennifer was still living with my parents at the time, and Jackie once managed to bring home a large crate of bananas, which he had shipped to her school.

When Jackie left for Montreal, I moved back into central London, managing to rent a large, four-bedroomed flat in Knightsbridge. I was nearly always lucky enough to live in nice parts of London, but we chose Knightsbridge because it was close to Harrods, where I had recently got a new job.

In those days, if you had any spare bedrooms you had to take in paying guests, such as officers normally stationed elsewhere who had been temporarily posted to London, usually to do staff work. This made for quite a lot of domestic work, as there were very few cleaning ladies indeed available in wartime.

I found myself saddled with two soldiers. Charles was a New Zealander, a paratroop captain who had lost a leg during the battle of Arnhem. Ray was also a captain – in the British army – who had been badly crippled and used crutches. I would cook for them and generally tidy up after them, and do their washing. I also had Vixen and Waffle to look after, and whereas Waffle was quite happy to stay in the flat, Vixen had to accompany me to work, which caused complications. Into this menage Jackie would periodically sail, dispensing his Canadian largesse, which was good news for Ray and Charles, though Charles was eaten up by a bitterness which he could never fully suppress.

At the time every able-bodied person had to have a job of some sort or other, but as my husband was still flying, on an overseas posting, the Ministry of Labour conceded that I should be available when he was home, and did not conscript me into one of the services. The local Labour Exchange directed me to a job at Harrods, as a salesgirl. I couldn't argue, though I wondered what on earth I was going to do with Vixen. When I was summoned to an interview designed to assess me and determine where in the store I would be of most use, I took her with me.

'I'm sorry, but we don't allow dogs,' the woman interviewer told me immediately.

I said: 'All right. I don't really want to work here anyway.'

'I didn't mean that,' she answered. 'I just meant that we don't allow dogs at the interviews.'

'Well,' I said, 'I wish I could have somehow known that in advance. What do you suggest I do with her, now that she's here?'

'Never mind that! We don't have time to worry about it. Tell me who you are. What can you do? Can you use a cash machine?'

I looked at her and said, 'No, I've never had to. I don't know anything about cash machines.'

'Well, you wouldn't be much good on the ground floor in the busy department.'

'It would appear not.'

She looked at me more closely. 'Would you mind standing up?' I did as I was asked and she looked me over. 'You've got a beautiful figure. I know what I shall do with you! I shall put you into the fur department as a model.'

That, I thought to myself, sounded a lot better than being a salesgirl; and more interesting than being stuck in something like haberdashery for the foreseeable future. Today I might have objected to such a job – but the fur trade then was free of the adverse publicity that animal welfare groups have now given it.

'Sounds fine,' I said. I had no experience as a model, but I thought I would soon pick it up. Vixen looked quite approving too.

'But you mustn't bring your dog, dear,' said the woman.

'Don't worry – I'll make arrangements. Anyway, don't you have kennels here?'

'Yes.' She sounded doubtful.

'Well, that's fine. I'll leave Vixen in the kennels during the day while I'm modelling, and collect her in the evenings.'

'I'm sure that could be arranged, but of course Harrods would not pay the kennel charge.'

I looked at her and asked, 'What will I be paid? Can I afford to keep Vixen here?'

'That is something you will have to discuss with the head buyer in the fur department – Mr Jacob.'

'Right-oh.'

She relaxed slightly. 'Good. Report for work tomorrow morning – and, dear, don't use the main entrance; there's an employees' entrance round the side.'

Vixen and I arrived the next day in good time. I'm always punctual. One of my good points. I left her in the kennels without any problem, and went over to the lifts to go up to the fur department. As I was getting in, one of the ground-floor buyers spotted me, and came up to say: 'Staff don't use the lifts! They use the escalators!' So I got out of the lift and crossed to the escalator. This, I thought, was not going to be for me.

However, when I reached the fur department I was confronted by an attractive girl with a lovely figure. Georgina was the other model in the fur department, and she was to become one of my greatest friends. Though we lost touch after Jackie and I left England, very recently I had a letter from her. She had seen me on television at the time of Jackie's kidnapping.

'Hello. I'm the new model.'

She smiled: 'Oh Christ, are you? Well, the first thing you'll have to do is introduce yourself to old Jacob!'

'Yes, I know. Where is he?'

'That's him over there – the fat one. I'm afraid it's rather like running the gauntlet.' She winked.

'Hold my hand and take me over,' I said.

Mr Jacob looked me up and down and pronounced judgement. 'Very nice,' he said. 'You'll be a good complement to Georgina, seeing as she's dark and you're fair.'

I looked round. 'What do I have to model?'

He spread his arms. 'The furs, dear. All sorts of furs.'

'And I'm afraid I need to know how much I'll be earning.'

Again he spread his arms. 'Well,' he said. 'That depends on your ability to sell the furs. You get a commission on your sales.'

I was nonplussed for a moment. 'Don't I get any basic salary?'

'We pay your bus fare.'

'I have a dog in the kennels here.'

He looked bewildered. 'What?'

'I have a dog in the kennels,' I repeated. 'She can't stay at home. I'd just like to know how she's going to be paid for.'

'Oh, is that all? Well, I dare say we might be able to stretch a point there and pay for your dog.'

That was the start of my modelling career, which lasted until we left England. I enjoyed it, and even became rather good at it. As for Vixen, she didn't have a bad time in the kennels, and when Jackie was home, she stayed with him. I was astonished at how many wealthy people there were in London still, even in wartime. They didn't let much get between them and their fun, and I made quite a good income. Sometimes it was a little difficult to keep a straight face when selling a coat. We would often get fat, elderly women in, and there Georgie or I would be, modelling a beautiful fur coat, a mink or a sable, and it would look good on either of us, because we had good figures and we were in our early twenties. The trick was to persuade our customers that they would look just as good, or better, and they almost always fell for it. I used to think, 'What do you suppose you'll look like, dear, waddling along in that, with your plump *derrière!*' Georgie and I had to avoid each other's eyes for fear of giggling. It was good that we were such great friends. As far as commissions went, we made about the same amount, and never had anything other than a friendly sense of rivalry between us.

Our only real problem was Mr Jacob, who thought he was God's gift to women. When we were trying on the coats before the customers arrived, to see how well they hung, he'd get us to parade up and down in front of him as he sat squeezed into a chair, and then he'd beckon us over, pretending that there was something wrong with the hemline. 'Bring the white lynx over here, dear!' Anything to get his hand up the inside of the coat. He was frightful, but essentially harmless. I was more interested in how smoothly Harrods managed to operate in wartime, and even to turn it to their advantage. One of our extra jobs was to look after and periodically air the vast number of furs which the very rich had left here in cold storage when they left the city at the outbreak of hostilities.

Harrods brought back one recent memory of the London air-raids. During the time that I had been an ambulance driver, I had managed to get a few hours off to do some shopping there, and I was in the store when suddenly the sirens went. The place was crowded with people. I was on the third floor, and my instinct was to get downstairs and out of the building as fast as possible, because I had a real fear of being closed in and having the building collapse on top of me. Two or three hundred of us were shepherded down to the basement of a building nearby, and I could feel myself becoming more and more nervous and upset. We all stood around silently in the semi-darkness, listening to the whining of the bombs as they fell. We were especially fearful of the parachute-bombs. Suddenly there was a massive explosion above us as one found its mark. It was followed by a thunderous noise of falling masonry and rubble that seemed to go on for ever, and then silence.

We remained standing in a communion of fright for what seemed an age longer before, very far away, we heard the all-clear sound; but our relief was swiftly replaced by panic as those nearest the staircases made to go up them.

'They're blocked! We're trapped!'

Nothing can convey a sense of the fear of being buried alive. I knew very well from experience that after a serious raid, with all the services stretched to the limit, it could be very many hours before we were discovered. And what if all the people who had seen us go into that basement had been killed? Who would know that we were there at all? No noise came from above after the loud sound of the all-clear. Nobody knew how we would get out or when rescuers might reach us. Those thoughts striking several hundred minds at once create an atmosphere which it is difficult to describe. I tried to make myself breathe slowly and regularly, resisting the urge to cry out.

Help came, but only after thirty hours. By that time I was a zombie. I'd gone past thinking. From that day on, the very idea of being in a crowd or in any enclosed space has brought me out in a cold sweat. If unavoidably I actually find myself in the situation, I can't move and I can't talk. I very quickly become hysterical, and yell and scream. That is why I dread being stuck in the lift when the electricity supply cuts out at home.

The war came to an end, and caught us, as it did so many people, on the hop. We were faced with the problem of what we were going to do. Jackie had not had time to develop a career before the war, and he had no training in anything but flying. While we were deciding what to do, he replaced 'Susan I' with 'Susan II', a newer version of the same MG, this time painted bright red; and poor Waffle passed away.

Like many pilots, Jackie's first thoughts turned towards running a pub. At the end of the war you could see clusters of ex-fliers in almost any bar coming to the same decision: pubs and bars were fun, associated with relaxation, and anyway none of these young men was qualified or experienced in business. At thirty-odd, entering the world of commerce filled them with foreboding. The alternatives, apart from running a pub, were few: an RAF career was open only to a tiny minority. There was the small but growing area of civil aviation, and there was airways administration; but most pilots baulked at desk jobs.

The idea of a pub became a fixation, but I was never keen on it. Meanwhile, we had a little money; Jackie had his demob pay, and I still had my modelling job. We had no dependants, for Jennifer continued to live in the country with my parents, and Vixen was as much at home with Wally as she was with us. We were footloose and fancy free – but only up to a point. And even if there was nothing to tie us to England, where else would we go?

4

BEIRUT 1946

We floundered about for a while, hoping that something would happen to make the decisions for us. Our first venture was of what I can only describe as the hairiest kind.

Jackie had fallen in with an ex-RAF crony in London called Solly. Solly, it emerged, not only knew a fair amount about boats and navigation, but also had a plan. Jackie was full of enthusiasm for this plan, but a shade vague about it when I asked him.

The next thing I knew, he and Solly had pooled most of their demob pay and bought a sixty-foot HDML with it. This large decommissioned boat, a Harbour Defence Motor Launch, to give it its full title, had been common during the war, but the Navy had no further need of so many of them. They were fast and roomy; but I was still hazy about what they proposed to do with it. I was furious that Jackie had sunk most of what we had into buying it.

When I finally heard what the plan was, I was even more angry.

'Smuggling cigarettes?'

'Hardly smuggling. Responding to a demand,' countered Jackie, unabashed.

'Is that what Customs and Excise will call it?'

'Look, they've got more than they can smoke in France. We've got hardly any here. Solly says that the profits we'll make on one trip will more or less pay for the boat.'

'It's black marketeering.'

'It's free enterprise. No one gets hurt, except the Excise, and two or three trips will buy us the time to really make plans.'

I was not convinced, and I was filled with dire forebodings of all of us getting caught and thrown into jail. But in the end I was carried along by the rest of them. We all had our allocated tasks: Solly was the captain, Jackie the engineer. Solly's wife was the cook, and I was the odd-job man.

On the day of the first trip, we drove down to the coast in 'Susan II'. Jackie was very worried that she might be stolen while we were away, and went to an inordinate amount of trouble parking her in a concealed spot. Then we carried our gear down to the boat. She looked very efficient and businesslike in the water, and my spirits rose slightly when we set off for Le Havre. The crossing passed without incident, though I think that once we were under way, everyone was a bit nervous of coming across a patrol boat. We weren't the only people engaged in cigarette-running, and Customs and Excise were well aware of what was going on.

My job at the other end was to jump off the bow of the HDML as we approached the harbour side, with a steel hawser over my shoulder, and belay it to a bollard. The quay was very slippery, and I didn't have proper shoes on. I jumped all right, but when I landed I slipped immediately and fell flat on my back. The hawser fell into the water, and the bow of the HDML veered out to sea again. I could hear shouting from the boat, and guessed that Solly was desperately trying to keep her head into the quayside, but I could neither see anything from where I lay, nor move. All this for a few hundred cartons of bloody cigarettes, I thought.

Jackie came to my rescue in the end, but I was injured badly enough to spend four days in hospital. I didn't think my experience augured at all well for our venture, but while I was laid up Solly got in touch with his contacts, and the cigarettes were loaded up successfully. As soon as possible, we started for home. I think the mood was cautiously triumphant.

It didn't last, of course. We were about halfway across the Channel when a patrol boat came up out of nowhere and made a beeline for us. Solly, whose courage deserted him rather abruptly, was all for dumping our load, but Jackie couldn't bear the thought. The cargo had used up the rest of our joint nest-egg, and the thought of the loss was unbearable. We were all in a desperate panic, and as we argued, the patrol boat drew closer and closer.

'Wait a minute,' Solly suddenly said. 'These things go like the wind once you open them up. What do you say we try to outrun her?'

We'd all been thinking, without much conviction, that we had better let the patrol boat catch up with us and then try to brazen it out, but this new idea had a swashbuckling ring to it that put our blood up.

'If they catch us then, we'll be buggered.'

'Whatever else we do now, we'll be buggered. Even if we ditch the lot, they're close enough to see us do it.'

'Then what are we waiting for?'

I don't know what kind of RAF officer Solly had been, but he was certainly a loss to the Navy. He opened the throttle steadily and as fast as he dared. The powerful engines responded smoothly and the huge craft shot across the water. The patrol boat must have been taken by surprise. They came after us, but before long even we realised that they would never catch us. When they were a speck on the horizon, we saw them turn away.

We brought our illicit cargo home safely, and sold it with great success. Solly was all for setting off again, but I'd had enough and put my foot down. We'd been lucky once, and recouped our investment – or near enough – and I wasn't about to repeat the risk of a spell in Holloway. I persuaded Jackie to side with me, and finally my argument carried weight with the others too. The Channel was, after all, stiff with patrol boats. We might have got away with it once more, but then a third trip would have been even more tempting, and sooner or later we would have been sure to be caught.

Exciting as that episode had been, we were back to square one. The pub idea surfaced again, but I still could not muster much enthusiasm for it. I went on modelling, and Jackie took Vixen for long, thoughtful walks, or visited the Royal Aero Club, where occasionally conversations could lead one in the direction of flying work.

It was there that he struck lucky, and the first span of the bridge to our new life was set in place. A man representing business interests abroad got chatting to him, and asked if he'd like to carry on flying. When Jackie said yes, the man wondered if the idea of flying freighter-Dakotas in the Mediterranean would appeal. They talked a little more, and agreed to meet again, more formally. Then Jackie brought the man home for drinks.

After some small talk, they told me that Jackie had been offered a job.

'But it means living abroad.'

'Where?'

'Cyprus.'

I hadn't been there, but I knew roughly where it was in the eastern Mediterranean. I knew, too, that, failing a pub, Jackie was keen to go on flying if he could. As I'd been the one to veto the pub idea, it seemed unreasonable to object to this too. Besides, the time was approaching when a job would become necessary. So I agreed.

'When do we leave?'

'In two weeks' time.'

That left a lot to be organised. Fortunately, the principal worry, posed by Jennifer's future, was easily solved. She would continue to live with my parents so that her education need not be interrupted. Vixen went to live with Wally, of whom she was already very fond. In the end, she spent the rest of her life with him – ten happy years. Wally also took care of 'Susan II', who was put into careful storage. There was no point yet in shipping out as if for ever. The job, which was to shuttle-fly to Tel Aviv with a mixed cargo of fruit and vegetables, was still an unknown quantity. We didn't know if we'd like it, or how long it would last.

My first impression of Cyprus was that I hated it, and that was largely because of the way they treated their animals. The horses were half-starved, and the most wretched of all were the poor beasts used to draw the buggies which served as taxis in those days. We found lodgings in a small hotel in Nicosia, where, in the days before partition, the island's principal airport was located.

The other thing I didn't like was the heat. It was the late summer of 1945. After England, it seemed unbearable, and still today in Beirut I detest the summer. The weather is impossible from July until October. Even if I were just there on holiday I would find it uncomfortable, but imagine ordinary day-to-day living. Imagine trying to iron in the humidity you get in Beirut. Every five minutes you feel you need to go and wring yourself out. Throughout the summer of 1989, on my own, trying to carry things up those five flights of stairs to my flat, I have come very close to defeat. I have cried and cried, alone in bed at night. You can't hold parcels, or the handles of bags – they slip in your hands because of the sweat. It is very frustrating. And then at the end of it you cannot refresh yourself with a shower or even a wash, because there isn't enough water, and I cannot carry a twenty-litre can up the stairs; it is simply too heavy. When I returned to Cyprus recently in connection with work on this book, the first thing I wanted to do was have a shower. I had looked forward to it all through the flight to Larnaca, and on the taxi drive to Limassol. We had reached the hotel when the friend who had accompanied me told me apologetically that there had been a change of plan, and we would have to return to another hotel, back in Larnaca. By the time I reached that shower, I wouldn't have relinquished it for a roomful of gold.

Jackie's job seemed fairly routine, but it started well. Seven or eight months passed quickly, and we were just beginning to get used to the place, and think about finding ourselves somewhere more permanent to live, when the trouble started. To this day I don't know exactly what it was, but it appeared that the aircraft which Jackie was flying backwards and forwards, to neither his knowledge nor mine, was carrying concealed arms to Tel Aviv. The first we knew about it was when the British Special Branch in Cyprus, who had obviously been monitoring the operation for some time, abruptly hauled Jackie in for questioning. He was thunderstruck, and he looked totally innocent, with his burnt face. He told the police the truth, which was of course that he had no idea of what had been going on.

'What did you think you were carrying?'

'Fruit and vegetables.'

'Is that all? Are you sure?'

'Of course.'

'Nothing ever struck you as odd – about the weight of the plane? The undercarriage?'

They went on like that for two days, before they finally decided that he was indeed innocent. His employer had been hiding machine-guns and other small arms in the undercarriage vault, which had been specially adapted. I was angry with the police. 'Good God,' I said, 'do you think, after everything he's done and been through in the war, that he's going to risk his whole life and career just for the sake of a handful of machine-guns? Anyway, is this the kind of money you'd expect for arms smuggling?' I showed them Jackie's pay-cheque. I realise now that if Jackie *had* been involved in any clandestine operation, the method of payment for it would not have been as straightforward as that, and the police must have known that too; but they believed us, and let him go. However, the owner of the Dakota was arrested and jailed, and the plane was confiscated, which left us out of a job.

The pay had not been high, and most of it had gone on our food and lodging. In fact, we were broke. We didn't even have the price of our tickets home. It was the kind of situation where something simply has to happen.

For a while it didn't look as if it would; but then someone we knew slightly came over on business to Cyprus from Beirut. Jackie happened to mention his problem over a drink, and our acquaintance immediately said, 'Why don't you come back to Beirut with me? Middle East Airlines are looking for pilots.'

Jackie was all for going right away – it really did seem like the answer to a prayer. Middle East Airlines was a small operation then, but everywhere after the war civil aviation was getting into its stride, based on the advances in aircraft technology made during the fighting. There was another possible side to the coin, however: a lot of out-of-work pilots chasing very few jobs.

We scraped together enough money for Jackie's flight to Beirut, but when we arrived at the airport the passport officer took one look at his passport and handed it back to him.

'Sorry,' he said. 'You can't go to Beirut with this.'

'Why not?'

'It's covered with Tel Aviv stamps.'

The delay caused by having to get a fresh passport lasted two weeks, and it was nerve-racking as we didn't know how long the queue for the MEA jobs would be. But finally the new passport came through, and Jackie set off.

Four days later he was back. 'I've got the job,' he said. 'And I start immediately. We'd better get packed.' Looking back, I think he must have made quite an impression. MEA in those days consisted of two Dakotas and two pilots – Jackie brought the strength up to three. We arrived at the tiny airport after a bumpy landing one sticky afternoon in the summer of 1946. My first impression of the place was not overwhelming, but I kept quiet, because I knew we needed the job. However, we were met by Selim Salaam, one of MEA's administrators, who was to become one of our dearest friends. Today he is the airline's managing director. He was enormously kind and helpful to us. As he arranged for our baggage to be collected, and bundled us into a car, he said, 'I've found you a flat. You don't have to have it if you don't like it; we'll go and look for something else instead. But this one has two advantages: the rent's low, and it's in a good area.'

The flat wasn't exciting, but it was certainly not bad, and it came furnished – at the time we hadn't a stick of our own. What made me fall for it was a detail: it had a large balcony, on which a huge camellia was growing – it was a small tree – and the scent of camellias wafting in from the balcony decided me.

'This is all right,' I said. 'We'll take it.' So we moved in, and christened it the Hovel. People were immediately friendly, and everyone connected with MEA came round to introduce themselves and bid us welcome. Gradually, as I began to pick up my first bits of Arabic, and as I got to know the city, I fell in love with Beirut and the Lebanon. Fifteen years of war haven't changed that. Beirut is beautifully placed between the sparkling sea and the peaceful green mountains. I used to walk along the Corniche by the sea as the sun was setting. There was a golden streak splashed across the water, and inland, the snowy tops of the mountains turned rose. If I had ever taken up painting, it is something I should have liked to try to get down on canvas.

Jackie quickly established himself as the best pilot, though he was still the most junior. It was not long, however, before he was approached to take one of the Dakotas on a mission for the Lebanese government. It had to be handled discreetly, for the job involved flying to Goa, on the west coast of India, and loading up there with gold bars for the Treasury. All the management of MEA at the time were pilots themselves, or had been, and one of them was to go with Jackie as his co-pilot.

The main problem concerning the mission was the length of the runway at Goa, which was only half a mile long. If on landing you failed to stop in time, you ended up in the sea. If you failed to reach take-off speed in time, you also ended up in the sea. When I heard about this, I hit the roof. Dakotas were lumbering planes and needed plenty of elbow room; neither

Jackie nor his co-pilot had any experience of taking off or landing in such a short distance, and on the return flight they would be very cargo-heavy. But Jackie, as usual, was all enthusiasm. 'Besides,' he pointed out, 'if I manage to pull this off, there'll be a considerable amount of good will, and a bonus.' I knew that there was no point in telling him that I'd gladly forgo both rather than have him risk his life. He had had a half-mile marked out on the runway at the aerodrome in Beirut, and he and his co-pilot practised take-offs and landings for a week before they were due to fly.

When the day came I could hardly speak for anxiety, but Jackie was his usual breezy self, and told me not to worry. They'd be gone for four days. If he could, he said he'd get a message through to me to say that they'd at least reached Goa safely. I heard nothing, and as the fourth day drew to a close, I felt gloom creeping up on me – though at the same time, curiously, I knew that nothing bad had happened. Jackie arrived in the evening, looking relaxed and grinning broadly.

'Mission accomplished,' he said.

It was clear to both of us that we had struck lucky. We liked the place, and Jackie loved the job. It was exciting to be in at the beginning of a new venture, in a new country. The war had left Europe overcast and in turmoil. Here, the sun shone nearly all the time; the cost of living was low, and the atmosphere was sophisticated and cosmopolitan. We thought we would be fools not to stay.

MEA took on two more pilots – North Americans – and bought two new planes. Jackie was promoted, and became the second most senior pilot. His salary went up gratifyingly. We began to feel cautiously affluent.

With that, and the bonus from the Goa flight, we were able to move into a flat which was far more a place of our own. We found it in Manara, then a lovely quarter of West Beirut, down by the sea; but now the scene of some of the fiercest fighting and bombardment. As there is a concentration of Syrian gun batteries there, the whole district presents a picture of blackened devastation today. We had three bedrooms and a big salon. Jackie, who has always been a good mechanic, and very good with his hands, decided that something special was needed to adorn our new home. But it was to be a surprise for me. For two or three weeks I was forbidden entrance to the spare bedroom, from which the noise of sawing and hammering came whenever Jackie was at home. Finally I was banished for a morning while whatever-it-was was put in position, and finishing touches applied.

When I came home, Jackie met me at the door. He was full of the pleasure of anticipation, just like a schoolboy – as he sometimes could be.

'Follow me to the door of the *salon*, and close your eyes.'

I obeyed, and he led me through the flat into the living room. He put his hands on my shoulders and gently put me in the right place.

'OK, you can open them now.'

It was beautiful. It was a bar, designed to fit in a corner of the room; but that wasn't all. Into its top, Jackie had fitted an aquarium, which ran its whole length. The aquarium had a glass top, so that when you sat at the bar with your drink, you could look down and see the goldfish swimming beneath you.

It became quite a talking point in Beirut. People would say that they were dropping round to the fish bar at the Manns'. But the sight of those fish swimming around was a bit hard on the people who'd had more than a few drinks!

The managing director of MEA then was Fawzi-el-Hoss. He was a very dynamic man and he wanted to expand the company in a big way, which he set about doing as soon as possible. During the next three years the airline increased in size to seven aircraft and eight or nine pilots. At the same time the chief pilot, who had always been a very heavy drinker, developed a stomach ulcer and was obliged to retire. By that time Jackie was acknowledged to be not only the best flier in MEA, but probably in the whole of the Middle East, and he was asked to take over the chief pilot's job. We had now very definitely arrived. However, MEA was also expanding its routes beyond those to Cairo and Nicosia. Dhahran had come onto the itinerary and Athens would soon follow. Jackie would frequently be away on one- or two-night stopovers, and I didn't see so much of him. In the meantime, I began to start work on what was to be a series of riding clubs and schools, which I have been involved in ever since and which still form the main interest of my life.

At that time, though, I was still involved with Jackie's work, in an indirect way. As the new flights introduced were growing longer, Fawzi decided that it was high time that refreshments were served on them. He asked me to organise something. All I could get was the tin lid of a biscuit box to serve as a tray, some plastic cups and spoons for Arabic coffee, and a modest selection of *mezza*. In the beginning I worked as a kind of unofficial air stewardess, and it was quite a job tottering up and down the aisle with my tray, as there was no pressurisation in the cabin in those days and the turbulence over the hot desert as we flew from Beirut over Saudi to Dhahran could be very vigorous. In fact, I have to admit I only did one trip in that direction myself, and it was quite enough for me. The flight took fourteen hours, and by the time I arrived I was a nervous wreck.

The ordeal didn't end with the flight. The local sheikh met us at the aerodrome, took one look at my blonde hair, which I have always worn quite long, and became very excited. He came over and seized my hair in his hands, which didn't look all that frequently washed, and gasped 'Gold, gold!' – the only English words he knew – in a kind of rapture. I thanked God that Jackie was the pilot on that flight. The crew climbed into his car and were driven to his home, where we were to stay overnight.

As we arrived, Jackie whispered, 'You might not be able to stay with the rest of us, you know.'

'Why on earth not?' I asked in a panic.

'You're a woman. They are all in strict purdah here.'

'But I'm not a Muslim; and in any case, I'm married!'

He grimaced. As it turned out, he was absolutely right. The sheikh led me off to the harem to join the other women. I spent a terrible night there, too scared to remove a stitch of clothing, and on the watch all the time in case he decided to come back for some more gold.

It wasn't long before MEA had the idea of introducing proper stewardesses, and I was presented with three promising girls for training. It was a bit like the blind leading the blind, but I think we made a good job of it. Not content with getting me to train the girls, they also asked me to design a uniform for them. This was something I enjoyed. As all the girls were dark, I wanted the uniform to be light, and I finally settled on pale blue. It was worn with a white blouse and a string tie, and a light blue forage cap with the MEA wings badge on it. I was very proud of it, and MEA used it for years – well into the time after the new international airport had been built, and MEA had replaced the Dakotas with jets, flying as far as Bombay and London. I think MEA got Hardy Amies to design the uniform the girls wear now: orange skirts and jackets, and yellow overalls.

We made a lot of friends very quickly, and our social life was full. We had a maid, we had some money, and we had fun. There were always cocktail parties, and the city was full of restaurants of every description offering every cuisine. Beirut was packed with foreigners then. There were pilots and diplomats, businessmen who would be over regularly from Europe for a couple of weeks at a time, and journalists. At first there were only three hotels. The St George's was modern, down by the sea. It had a large marina, where the wealthy Lebanese kept their yachts and speedboats. In town there was a smaller place called the Normandie, and there was one Arab hotel, the Ma'Haba.

Much of it seems like a dream now. I remember that before the wars the local fishermen used to take huge nets out in rowing boats and let them down into the sea in the late evening. The following morning they would return with twenty extra pairs of hands to haul the nets in, and that was a splendid sight, at dawn, with the sunlight only just touching the sea. The little silver fish glittered and flashed in the sun as they jumped in the nets. When the wars started, the fishermen stopped using their overnight nets because of the shelling, and started using dynamite instead. That was terrible. They'd blow the fish to hell and then just scoop them all up quickly in nets. But most people wouldn't buy them, because they were killed so fast that they weren't fresh by the time they got to market. Eventually, the Tourism Ministry, which still existed when this was going on, banned the practice. They didn't think it was good for Lebanon's image that the few tourists who were still coming should see it.

The fishermen went back to their old way. I was down on the beach with my poodle Tara recently in the morning when they were pulling the big nets in, hauling on the ropes and singing. Tara was fascinated by the sight of hundreds of men dragging at nets full of fish. They'd almost got the first net ashore when the shelling started. I grabbed Tara and ran, looking back over my shoulder as I fled. The men had abandoned the nets and were running for cover. The fish were still in shallow water, and you could see them jumping up, trying to get back into the sea.

There were idyllic moments in the early days, and I don't regret having had them, even though I am having to pay for them now. One Christmas Day at the very beginning, we had spent the morning swimming in the sea with our friends Pat and Peter Brooke before lunching at the St George's. When lunch was over, Peter, who was a great sportsman, suggested we work off our food by going skiing. I hadn't skied before, and neither had Jackie, but it seemed a good idea. We climbed into the car and drove up to Ferayah. The journey only takes an hour and a half, and I don't know of many other places in the world where you can swim in a warm sea before lunch and ski in the mountains afterwards.

That day we tinkered about, but we tried again later on less full stomachs. I remember that we arrived in Ferayah at about eleven in the morning, and hired our wooden skis and leather boots. It was a glorious day; the snow sparkled, and the air had that lovely crisp quality that makes you feel glad to be alive. We started on the beginners' slopes to warm up. Jackie and I were very much novices. I began to get the hang of it, but Jackie, who'd had perhaps a couple more tumbles than me, decided after an hour that he'd had enough, and announced that he was going down to the tavern to sample the beer. Peter and Pat and I went on.

After a while, Peter said, 'As you seem to be taking to this, would you like to try something a little more interesting?'

'Yes, sure,' I said. I was always game for anything.

We took the next ski lift, which took us to a downhill run punctuated with intermittent trees.

'What about the trees?' I asked.

'They're no problem,' said Peter, and taught me how to do a fairly simple turn, which I mastered. Then Pat started, and told me to follow her down, since I didn't know the route.

We started off splendidly, and I felt wonderful. My confidence soared. But then I missed an important tree, passing it to the right instead of the left. Still, that didn't seem to be so bad. In front of me was a lovely stretch of snow, which clearly no one else had been on. I let myself go, and started to fly down it.

Pat and Peter had noticed my departure from the beaten track, and now Peter came charging after me. 'Sunnie!' he yelled. 'Stop!'

Stop, I thought; what for? This is gorgeous. So I went on.

'Stop, for Christ's sake!' bellowed Peter, gaining on me. 'Stop, you silly fool, or I'll push you over!'

As I refused to stop, he swung round in front of me and indeed pushed me over. We both glared at each other. Then he pulled me up and showed me, a few yards further on, a sheer drop to the bottom of the mountainside, of about a thousand feet.

We knew we'd 'arrived' when we got an invitation to the Beards' New Year's Eve party. He was English, she was

Lebanese, and they had two sons, one of whom later married an English girl called Beth. Their money came from a transport company, Nairns, which among other things at the time ran air-conditioned buses over to Saudi Arabia; this was well before the days of flights there out of Beirut. I never travelled that way myself, and wouldn't have for all the tea in China. They were a delightful family, and every year they gave a gala dinner, followed by dancing. You really felt you had made it in Beirut society if you got an invitation.

The party was held in the huge garden of their villa. The whole place was illuminated with coloured lights, and dominated by a gigantic Christmas tree. It would start at ten o'clock, and people would arrive soon after for cocktails and snacks. Dinner followed at tables laid all around the garden, and usually there were about a hundred guests. At midnight, we would see the New Year in with paper hats, balloons and dancing. We were foolish in those days! It would all come to an end around four or five in the morning, and as it started to get light, a group of us would go down to the harbour and have breakfast there as the sun rose behind the mountains and made the sea dazzling.

Nearly all the family is dead now. Mme Beard died of cancer, and the father and both the sons were killed in the shelling. Beth got away to England with her two children, and she has stayed there, I believe. I have never seen her again.

Once we'd decided to make a permanent home in Beirut, there were a few practical matters to deal with in England. Jackie had, after much soul-searching, decided not to have 'Susan II' shipped out to Lebanon, and asked Wally to sell her. We bought a sensible VW Beetle with left-hand drive, but after a while, Jackie began to miss his sports car. In the summer of 1949, we were due a few weeks' leave, and returned to England to see our families. Social duties behind us, we found ourselves back in London, and Jackie said, 'I've had an idea.'

He proposed to buy a new MG sports car – 'Susan III' – and drive it back to Beirut over the three weeks we had remaining. It was a plan I was glad to fall in with, and the overland route through Europe with 'Susan III' that summer was unforgettable. We dawdled, spending far too long in Paris, and taking detours to Rome and Venice before heading east through Yugoslavia, Greece and Turkey, and so home. In Lebanon, Jackie drove 'Susan III' for many happy years, before selling her in her old age to a young Lebanese who was crazy about her. I stuck to the VW.

In Paris, Jackie bought me a Hermès forward-seat jumping-saddle. It is the best that money can buy. I still have it, and still use it, though I shudder to think how much it would cost to buy new, today. He might not have liked horses much himself, but he knew that riding was in my blood, and that seeds had already been sown in Lebanon which would grow into what was to be my lifetime career.

5

TEACHING THE LEBANESE TO RIDE

At heart I'm very English – not British; English, and proud of it. In England I had a few months of riding before the Second World War started. If you ride in Rotten Row, as I used to, frequently, you have to be correctly dressed. You would buy a black hunting jacket, because only international show jumpers are allowed to wear red jackets with different coloured collars. So normally it is black for England, and green for Ireland. In those days the place to go for your jacket was Moss Bros, which had a large department just for riding clothes.

The most important part of one's dress, however, is one's bowler hat, and for that one never goes anywhere but to Mr Lock's in Piccadilly. In Lebanon, many American riders would wear bowlers, but theirs were always rather wide-brimmed; they looked a little like stetsons. The English bowler is very narrow-brimmed and neat. The top echelon wore bowlers with a white lining. A brown lining meant that the hat had been bought off the peg; but if you had your hat specially made for you, it was lined in white. Mine always had a white lining. Your jodhpurs were white for showjumping, and beige for other occasions. Boots were black-topped, unless you were a Master of Fox Hounds or a particularly distinguished hunter – then you could wear brown tops.

I've thrown my English boots away because in Beirut it's impossible to wear leather during the winter: the rain is so heavy, and the floods can be so bad, that you have to wear wellingtons, otherwise you simply can't walk around. In the summer, it's too hot to wear proper breeches, so I generally put on a pair of light slacks, with American chaps over them. That's ideal, especially with the water shortage, because the chaps keep your trousers clean while riding, and when you take them off afterwards there's no need to change if you're going on to do, say, some shopping afterwards.

As for my bowler, I bought it at Lock's about fifteen years ago; but I refuse to throw it away, even though it is faded, and bashed and dented where my head has come into contact with walls or fences or horses' feet. I feel that it's lucky, and as I have always been a superstitious person, I won't change it, though Jackie has frequently offered to pay for a replacement whenever I get a chance to visit Lock's again. I'm keeping it until one of us – it or me – falls to pieces. The worst dent is in the front, and it happened when we were in the process of buying a horse on behalf of one of the members of our riding club. An animal was brought in for us to try out and, as always, I had to be the guinea-pig. I managed to get on, but only just, for the horse was very nervy and kept dancing about, pulling his back legs under his body. He obviously did not want anyone on his back.

The grooms who had brought the horse along had forgotten to tell me – either by accident or design – that the minute you were in the saddle, he would go off at a full gallop round the ring. I wasn't expecting this at all – you never go faster than a canter in a ring – but despite the fact that he was a new and unfamiliar horse I wasn't too perturbed to start with, as I'd learnt the old race-track trick of pulling the rein up on one side and down on the other – you can generally stop any horse like that. However, when I tried it, it had no effect whatsoever – he just kept on going. Then I began to get nervous because at the far end of our ring there's a big stone wall. I managed to get him round two circuits, but at the third he suddenly changed his leading leg, and that put me off balance. I shot off his back and slammed into the stone wall. If I hadn't been wearing my lucky hat I would have been killed.

Needless to say, we didn't buy the horse.

My involvement with riding clubs started by chance, though I took up riding again almost as soon as we were settled in Lebanon, which is a country with a great equestrian tradition. The Arab strain here was once among the purest in the world, though nowadays breeders worry about its dilution through interbreeding with English and other stock – another unfortunate by-product of the war, since although horses now change hands for very high prices, in most cases the dealers are Bedouin opportunists taking advantage of the semi-anarchic situation. There are no horse fairs, no supervised dealing, and little properly supervised breeding.

Jackie bought me my first horse. He was called Antar, after an Arab god of strength, and he was a four-year-old stallion, bred for racing. In the beginning, a few enthusiasts formed a very loose club – it was more an informal regular gathering for rides over the dunes and along the beaches. We held an annual Boxing Day 'meet' in the English tradition, but we would either have a drag hunt or play 'Hare and Hounds'. The hares would get a five-minute start. In those halcyon days one could ride for miles without seeing a building and it was superb, exhilarating and fun. To be considered 'killed', a hare had to be tapped on the shoulder by a hound, and it's easy to imagine the twists and turns of the hares to avoid that fate. We even rode right into the sea to elude capture.

I remember that at the time a Hungarian was riding with us. His name was Frigis, which I thought sounded gorgeous. At one of our meetings he suggested a game of 'Hare and Hounds', with a country pub we all knew as our *but de voyage*. We rode out across the open land where the international airport is now, galloping madly after each other, until we came to a little forest which lay near to where the old golf course used to be. I turned into the forest to avoid one of the 'hounds', who had spotted me. Unfortunately, nobody knew that the Lebanese army had turned the forest into an assault course for troop training; it was full of obstacles and hidden pitfalls. My horse and I charged down a steep slope and both of us promptly fell into a huge hole that they'd dug. The horse was all right, but I broke my leg.

I started yelling my head off. Eventually some of the others came up. It was a terrible business to get me out with a broken leg, though the horse managed to scramble free up a steep slope. My friends lowered themselves down and made a human ladder, one standing on another's shoulders, and very precariously they managed to hand me out of the pit that way. They put me on a quiet horse, and took me to the local hospital. The doctor in charge there, Fouad Khoury, got to know me very well over the years. As I'd be brought in with my latest bash, he'd look up and say, 'Not you again!'. I've broken almost every bone in my body in my time. You can't ride the way I have – showjumping and racing – without getting knocked about a bit.

Showjumping was something I took up in Lebanon, and though I'd never done it before, I found myself winning cups quite regularly before long. In all, I won seven cups for racing and jumping, and an eighth cup was a special award for the Best Horsewoman in Lebanon, of which I am very proud. It has survived, along with the racing cups, but the jumping cups were all destroyed during the Israeli invasion, when a shell blew half our flat away. It landed outside the building, but the force of its explosion caused the windows on the street side to blow in and the ceilings to collapse. All the trophies and all the photograph albums that were in the *salon* were destroyed. The cups which survived happened to be in Jackie's room on the other side of the apartment. Jackie preferred to sleep alone on occasion because of the discomfort the heat caused to his skin grafts.

When I started my first proper club, and began to train girls to enter competitions, I gave up showjumping myself, but I raced as an amateur for two seasons in the late fifties and early sixties.

I remember the first – purely amateur – race very well. There were two women jockeys – Carol Selby, who has also been in touch with me recently after a long absence from my life, and myself. She and I were the only women riders experienced enough for the job. We wore our own clothes – not colours – and rode our own horses that first time, which were jumpers, not racers. The start was right by the entrance gate to the course, and the race was over one and a half circuits. Our mounts refused to come up to the tape, but our embarrassment was spared by the fact that the starter couldn't get *any* of us amateurs into a straight line.

I remembered that day, thirty years ago, as I passed by the race-course recently. I was crossing back from the East Side, and there was, briefly, an opportunity to clamber into the stadium and have a look round. The race-course is devastated now, together with the French ambassador's residence, which is close by. It used to be beautiful; I'd been to the residence often in the past as a guest, for the ambassador's daughter, Christiane, was one of my star riders. It is tragic to see it now, a bombed-out shell. All the walls are pock-marked by bullets, and the stables have been flattened. I looked around the stands and remembered the time when they were filled with cheering, happy people. I remembered the long uphill finishing stretch. I will not go back for a second look. It is too sad.

That first race was invigorating. It was the first amateur event they had staged, and no one knew how it would go. The director of the course, Gabriel Trahd, was a strict Muslim, and we knew that he was terrified that the ordinary people down in the big public enclosure by the start would not like the idea of women riding and would make trouble for us. At that time such a thing was simply not done, and it had taken a lot to persuade him to let us ride in the first place. In the event, the crowd loved us, and clapped and cheered. I still tingle when I think of the excitement of coming up to the finish; and yet all you could see out of the corner of your eye as you dashed past were the bookies waving their arms.

Everyone agreed that the amateur race had been a great success, and the course committee were happy to put on one a month thereafter as a regular event. Their one stipulation was that we should ride proper racehorses, not our own jumpers. Each of us was duly attached to a stable, and I rode, at his request, for Henri Pharon, then one of the country's top breeders. I felt terrific the day I first put on his colours. The only problem was the lead I had to carry in my saddle to handicap the horse, as I am slim and small. It was more of a handicap than mere weight, too, for it was dead weight, and sat to the back of the animal. Of course I stood in my stirrups like everyone else and pushed my own weight forward, but it was hard going, so I came to the conclusion that I'd rather use my own, heavier Hermès saddle than a leaded racing saddle. That made a difference. I even won several races. People began to bet on me. And that was my undoing, because women were not supposed to outdo men. I was envied, and I had to be brought down.

One day I was riding the favourite, a black horse called Barbary, whom nobody else would touch. He had great spirit, but, like most black horses, a filthy temper to go with it.

'Hold him in until the final stretch, then give him his head and he'll win it for you,' Mr Pharon told me. I said I'd try. I took him up to the start and he reared a couple of times, but I'd expected this and stayed on, telling him to stop waving to the crowds. He came to the line, and we were off. At first it was fantastic; we hugged the group right round. The last couple of furlongs were approaching when I began to sense that all was not well – I gave him his head, but far from surging forward, he began to trail. We came in last. People were booing and yelling; they'd lost money though they'd bet on a certainty.

In the enclosure I asked Mr Pharon what precisely he thought had gone wrong. 'I've no idea,' he said. 'I don't understand it. He's a bit unruly, but he's an excellent horse.'

'He wasn't excellent today.'

The truth wasn't far to seek. Barbary had been doped. Clearly a rival stable had had enough of seeing me win and wanted to discredit me. They succeeded. The next time out, I was booed from the start. The fun of it all, which is what we'd been doing it for, had been killed. I was very disheartened, and pulled out, taking the other women jockeys with me – and by that time there were a few of us besides Carol and me. They tried to continue the event in a hashed sort of way with amateur jockeys riding against professionals, but it didn't work. We were the ones who had drawn the crowds.

Thinking of Barbary, I am reminded of another experience with a black horse, though it is a tragic one. A delightful retired naval captain named Kenneth Lyle lived in Beirut in the early days, and though he was sixty-odd he was still a good rider. He had ridden to hounds in England, and wanted to keep up the exercise. He started with us on one of the club horses, but after a while decided that he'd like an animal of his own, and asked me to look out for one. I finally came across a beautiful black stallion. I really fell for him, and despite knowing the reputation that blacks have, I knew Ken was a good rider, and I told myself that, after all, there are some black horses with quite sweet natures. This may have been against my better judgement, for the general rule with Arabian horses is; the darker the colour, the more dangerous the animal. The best ones for children or beginners are whites or greys, or even chestnuts. But at all costs avoid blacks and bays. And the black I'd found had a further disadvantage.

I hedged my bets at first and showed Ken a couple of other mounts, which he liked, but found dull.

'I'd like something with a bit more spirit, if it's possible.'

I said, 'Well, there is one I've found. He's a beauty, but I have to tell you that not only is he black, but he's only got one eye.'

Ken was as shocked as I had been. 'Good God,' he said, 'what happened to him?'

Cruelty to animals was something I had had to get used to in Lebanon. 'I understand from the man who's selling him that he once gave his previous owner a bit of trouble. The man decided to teach him a lesson and took his whip to his head. He whipped him so severely that he took out one of his eyes.'

Ken was silent.

'Do you think you could handle a horse that's been treated like that?' I asked.

'I don't know, but I'd love to have a look at him.'

I brought him round to the club, and Ken, naturally, got me to ride him round a bit first. He was beautiful, a delightful ride, and no problem at all. Ken took over and after two or three circuits he said; 'I'll buy him.'

Not long afterwards, Ken had to go to London on naval business and he stabled Midnight – as he had christened the horse – with me. He behaved perfectly, was always gentle, loved his sugarlumps, and never tried to kick or bite when you went into his box to muck out.

One day, after I had finished exercising him on the dunes, I decided to make a detour on the way back through a village where you could buy particularly delicious honey. Then we came down part of the main road back to the club, and I was walking Midnight because the road surface was slippery after rain. Suddenly a petrol tanker drove up behind us and stayed there. The driver thought it was the greatest fun to blow his horn continually at Midnight in the hope that I'd be thrown off. He drove right up beside the horse and hooted loudly. Even then, we might have avoided damage, but the bastard was on Midnight's blind side, and of course the horse could only hear the noise and sense threat. He reared in panic, threw me, lost his balance, and fell backwards on top of me. The lorry driver sped off – he'd had his little thrill.

Midnight broke his back and had to be destroyed. In the fall, I broke my leg, which wasn't too bad as it was a clean break and soon healed up; but I also smashed two vertebrae, which still give me trouble today. That damage also put paid to any more showjumping. Middle East Airlines flew me to England to see a specialist, who patched me up, but forbade me ever to ride anything other than a quiet horse again. The slightest jar, he said, could put me in a wheelchair for life.

We try not to ride along roads in Lebanon. Lorries and cars still like to play that kind of trick.

Ken was wonderful about the incident. Not long afterwards, when the Mountbattens visited Lebanon, he arranged for us not only to be invited to cocktails aboard their cruiser, but also to be among the eight who were invited to remain for dinner. In those days, I have to say, one bounced back from any disappointment or adversity. Jackie and I were a popular couple, and the social round swept us along for years on a joy-ride which I suppose both of us assumed would last for ever. How wrong we were.

I started my first proper club at the suggestion of our skiing friends, Pat and Peter Brooke, who were also keen riders. I managed to scrape together a little capital, found a useful site to rent in the Bir Hassan district of Beirut, engaged workmen to build me some stables, and set out with another riding friend, Sammi Assab, to look for a couple of good-natured horses to start us off. Sammi had told me that many of her friends, and their children, would love to learn to ride if only they had the opportunity; I thought, correctly as it turned out, that we had identified a hole in the market, and I had no objection to enjoying myself and making a bit of money at the same time. Jackie had absolutely no objection to that, but apart from handling the catering and the drinks at club get-togethers from time to time, he never showed the slightest interest in what I did. That suited me fine. In the early days, he was preoccupied with flying and his own flying friends.

The main difficulty in looking for horses locally was that Arab horses are temperamental and highly strung. At that time, too, none was gelded, because the Lebanese believed that gelding robbed them of spirit, so that one could only acquire stallions;

there were mares, too, of course, but stallions and mares do not sit well together, especially when the mares are in season. Only very recently, we had to let a stallion called Shyal go, because he got far too frisky at such times. The children would look at him round-eyed, and say to me: 'Mrs Mann, what can the matter with Shyal be?' I told them, 'He's just feeling a bit off-colour today, dears.'

Sammi and I struck lucky when we discovered that a touring circus from Germany had gone bankrupt and was selling its disposable assets, including all the livestock except the elephants. We went along and bought Togo and Strauss. They were a delightful pair of ponies. Togo was piebald, and Strauss skewbald. They were the founder members of what came to be known as the Horse and Pony Club.

Although they had very gentle natures, and were well used to being handled, they had never been ridden. Strauss's job, as his name partly implies, was to do a little dance, and Togo had been the leader of the troupe of performing horses. To our relief, they objected neither to the saddle nor to people sitting on them, although they each had particular idiosyncrasies, which I discovered in a dramatic fashion. The first horror came when one small child, aged about seven, was on Togo. It was a very hot day, and I lifted my hand up to pull the brim of my hat further down over my eyes. To my amazement and perturbation, Togo promptly stood up on his hind legs, and off came the child – luckily a fearless little creature who bounced comfortably onto the soft sand. All Togo had done was obey orders – I realised that a raised hand to him was a signal to perform this particular one of his repertoire of party tricks. After that, we had to be extremely careful to keep our hands well down near Togo.

Strauss showed his peculiarity in an even more strenuous way. It has always been our custom on certain days for everyone who is experienced enough to leave the ring to go out for a long promenade among the dunes. Back in the fifties, Beirut was at its best, and you could ride across open country by the sea all the way south to Khalde. One day we were out riding in this way with five or six children, when I suddenly saw Strauss draw up. His eyes were fixed on the horizon, and, to my alarm, his ears went straight back. I followed his gaze and saw, in the distance, a caravan of half a dozen camels slowly ambling inland with their drovers. I hadn't time to react further, because at that moment Strauss snatched the reins from his small rider's hands, turned, and made a dash for home. I couldn't believe my eyes, as he'd always been so quiet and well-behaved, but I set off after him at a gallop, straining to keep up. There was no way I could catch the reins as he'd pulled them over his head, but luckily the little boy on his back kept calm and clung to his mane like grim death. We hurtled on for what seemed ages with no let up until we reached the club. Strauss charged through the gates, then paused, looked back once, and lowered his head. The ears pricked back up. I dismounted quickly and went over, lifting the exhilarated little rider off. Strauss was as quiet as a lamb. It never happened again, but then, he never saw any more camels. I think he must have been bitten by one during his circus career.

I was the first European, and the first woman, to run a riding club in Lebanon, and I knew that there were people who looked on me askance; certainly I had had my share of difficulties when applying for an operator's licence. But the place grew quickly and membership was full well before the end of the first year. Many people bought their own horses, which they would stable with us, necessitating the building of more boxes and the hiring of more grooms. Everyone's sights were on showjumping, and in the end we established a special advanced class to that end. My four star pupils were the daughters of the French and North American ambassadors, Christiane de Boisseson and Kathy Mayer, Margaret Kadam and Ada Alamuddine.

One thing I'm rather proud of was that I got the children to look after the horses as well as ride them. Wealthy Lebanese children were not accustomed to doing any work for themselves at all, and they rather enjoyed the novelty of it. They loved mucking out, fetching water and weighing feed. It also taught them that horses were not to be taken for granted; but because they were unused to the experience, there were amusing moments. A child whom I had finally persuaded to summon up the courage to give a horse a sugarlump gasped, 'Oh, Mrs Mann, what shall I do? My hand's dirty – it's sticky from the sugar.' I'd say, 'Of course it is – go and wash it in the bucket over there.' Slowly, they learned. It wasn't until the war started, though, that they finally realised that they were not little golden gods.

The club expanded so fast that we had to find some horses to join Togo and Strauss, and I wanted a couple of good mounts to enter in the showjumping competitions we had our eye on. Among my friends was Captain Victor Khoury, who ran the Lebanese Army Equestrian Team. Victor went on to become a general. Now retired, he still trains horses to the east of the city.

It turned out that Victor had a number of partially trained Arab horses which were being replaced on the army team by foreign stock in time for the Middle East championships, which were being held in Cairo that year. I went to look at them with him, and bought several. One of them was called Ibn-el-Tyr, which means 'flight of a bird'. As French is the second language of Lebanon, and as so many of my club members were European, I rechristened him 'Oiseau'. He lived up to his name: as a jumper, he flew over everything. He had already won several races, and Victor had also jumped him. He said he would not sell him to anyone else but me, because he knew I would not maltreat him or sell him to a carter when he grew too old to work. This cruel fate befell many retired racehorses and jumpers.

Apart from pedigree strains, horses were treated very badly in Lebanon, especially cart horses. They were frequently starved and beaten. In the Sabra camp in the early eighties there was a clique of carters and horse traders, made up of particularly brutal men; most of them were killed during the Phalangist attack on the camp during the Israeli invasion. To become a cart horse was a dreadful fate for a former racehorse. Carts were, and are, a principal mode of transport, particularly for hauling kerosene, but pulling a cart is alien to a racehorse's experience, and petrifying, since to him a cart is something heavy and lumbering which is following him, which he can't escape, but which never quite catches him. One man, the leader of the Sabra clique, called Abed, used to take the new horse, shackle it between the shafts despite its panic, then drive it with a whip in the heat of the day into the heavy sand dunes, and there beat it until it dropped from exhaustion between the shafts, to break its spirit. That's how they used to train them to pull the carts.

At about the same time that I acquired Oiseau, I bought a splendid mare from a top local trainer called Fistock. This horse, whose Arab name was Johara, was rechristened the French equivalent, 'Bijou'. On her, Christiane de Boisseson was to take the Lebanese showjumping world by storm. By the time we entered Bijou in competition, three rival clubs had opened and flourished, but Bijou was able to beat all-comers, even the army team, which scarcely pleased Victor! Unfortunately, our success also excited envy, which once again led to problems for me.

A new equestrian centre had been established at the City Sportive, an enormous sports complex in Beirut. It was equipped with an international standard jumping ring, and three other smaller rings, and it housed the army team's horses, together with those of the three other Lebanese-run clubs. Jumping competitions there became frequent, but I kept my riders training on our home ground. It was the usual tactic – one hides one's best until one is ready to show it. When we did enter there, our results were spectacular, with Christiane and Bijou winning two of the major events on no less an occasion than the Twenty-One Nation Show against the best of Lebanese and foreign competitors. I was indescribably proud and excited. In the audience were the President, Camille Chamoun, himself, and the Commander-in-Chief of the Army, General Adel Chehab.

After that, we went from strength to strength, competing in many inter-Lebanese shows and always coming away with a first or second rosette. I trained Christiane Boisseson and Margaret Kadam, on Bijou and a stallion called Dehi respectively, to do double-jumping in unison. It is a very difficult exercise, particularly with stallions and mares, which are inclined to fight if they are brought too close together; but Dehi was a lazy, easy-going horse, and Bijou always had perfect manners. We put on the demonstration and it worked perfectly, the two girls soaring over the specially widened jumps together in absolute harmony. I was too pleased to be aware of one or two tight-lipped expressions among the audience. The Horse and Pony Club was being spoken of as the best in Beirut.

Meanwhile, I had been looking for a rider for the lovely Oiseau. I found her in a young English girl called Jacky Brown, whose father was the representative for De Havilland in Lebanon. She was about fifteen then, and at boarding school in England, where she also rode; but she would come out in the school holidays to be with her parents. She was enchanted when I suggested that she ride Oiseau, and the two of them hit it off splendidly – they were made for each other. After a time, I decided to enter them for a competition at the City Sportive, and it was there that disaster struck.

They had done a clear round up to the water jump. There, Oiseau misjudged the take-off, getting too close to the water, and putting one foot into it. This made him panic and he jumped hastily, slipping, and then landing on his head on the edge of the concrete basin. Jacky was thrown clear, and was all right apart from a couple of bruises; but it was the start of a tragedy for Oiseau. Nobody knew at the time that there was anything wrong with him, and in fact Jacky remounted and took him over two more jumps to complete the course. Afterwards, I rested him for three days because I could see that he'd had a shock, but when we tried him out again, he behaved just like a novice. Instead of approaching the jumps as he had done, he backed away from them in fear; and when he could be coaxed into jumping, he blundered and knocked over the poles.

This wasn't Oiseau any more – he had been a horse who adored jumping, you could almost say that he lived to jump. Show him a jumping ring, and his ears would go up and his eyes brighten. Something was terribly wrong.

The *Daily Mail* correspondent in Beirut at the time, Arthur Cook, was a friend of mine, and he suggested that an ophthalmic surgeon acquaintance of his should come and have a look at the horse. When the surgeon had done so, our worst fears were confirmed: Oiseau was going steadily blind. It would take a week before his sight was completely gone, but nothing could reverse the process. Everyone was in tears – Jacky, myself, even the grooms. We all loved Oiseau. He used to put his head on your shoulder whenever you stood near, and gaze at you soulfully. That sort of horse. But what could we do with him? What would be kindest? I couldn't bring myself to have him put down, and in any case, in himself he was strong and fit. I decided to try riding him myself.

To my slight surprise and great relief, the experiment succeeded. I found that he was very responsive to the touch of reins and legs. He soon became confident enough in my hands to trot. I rode him for two months or so, and then, as Jacky had had to return to school in England, I gave him to Arthur Cook's young daughter to ride. Anna was marvellous with him. She trotted him round the ring, and soon brought him up to a canter. Then I decided to take things a stage further, and had a small jump – no more than a foot high – placed in the ring.

Arthur was worried about Anna. 'Are you sure this is wise? She's not going to get killed, is she?'

'No,' I said. 'She'll be all right.'

Anna guided Oiseau round to the jump, gave him a little squeeze with her legs, and said, 'Up!' Over they went – perfectly. Everybody clapped and cheered, and I think we all felt marvellous. From there we progressed slowly on to ever larger jumps, and finally we entered the pair of them in a modest competition – which they won. No one knew that Oiseau was blind until after the event. When I told them, he got a standing ovation. He went on to win two more competitions before I retired him at the age of fifteen. He finally died peacefully in his sleep. Arthur Cook published an article in the *Daily Mail* under the title 'The Faith of a Woman and the Courage of a Horse'. Oiseau is the only horse I have ever heard of who was successfully taught to jump again after going blind.

The pleasure I derived from teaching so many delightful adults and children to ride cannot be adequately described, but my success had created enemies for me, and I had been too involved in my work to pay them any attention. Now, after three years, when the time came for me to renew my licence, they struck.

I knew that conservative elements in town were not pleased that a foreign woman should be giving instruction in riding to men – that was considered most *infra dig* – but I had no idea of the degree of envy my success had stirred up. The envy was motivated by business pragmatism too – the Horse and Pony had a waiting list; the other clubs which had started up were still looking for members. My licence renewal application was refused. When I asked why, I was told quite simply that they were sorry, but they couldn't issue licences to foreigners any more – there were Lebanese clubs and instructors now; English ones were no longer needed.

6

TERROR

The grounds of the Horse and Pony Club were taken over by a Lebanese instructor. However, the core members of my club wanted to stay with me, and it seemed a pity if nothing could be saved from such an unnecessary wreck. Although I could no longer operate a public club without a licence, there was nothing to stop me running one privately.

At the time of the demise of the Horse and Pony Club, Jackie and I were living in a large rented villa nearby, with its own garden, having moved up in the world from our Manara flat. I took my five best horses, including Bijou, and moved them to our garden, got permission from the villa's owner to have some boxes built for them, and managed to rent an adjacent field, where we constructed a ring. Jackie and I have always loved dogs, and at the time we had several, including half a dozen strays who had billetted themselves on us. The logical name for the new club, therefore, was the Horse and Hound.

The Horse and Hound Club lasted four very happy years, but once again, success was our undoing; for in the space of that time our membership grew and grew, to the point where it was no longer possible to pass ourselves off as a private club. Worse, we were beginning to attract people away from rival clubs. Our fate was, therefore, sealed once more. I was told that I could not operate on such a scale without a licence, and I was also told that I could not have one.

By now, however, I was well known, and had many friends in Lebanese riding circles. If I could not have a licence myself, there were plenty of other people who could, and who were willing to give me house-room. Two things happened. The core of the membership of the Horse and Hound Club was taken over by a great ally and former member, Kamal Farajellah, and his Swedish wife, Leonie, who were both keen riders. They managed to acquire a splendid piece of land at Bir Hassan, not far from the original Horse and Pony. They called their new establishment the Arabian Horse Club, and it is still there, although sadly it is long since that Kamal and Leonie went their separate ways. She now lives in Sweden with their children, and he is in London, and has remarried; though he retains an interest in the club. But the Arabian Club is my base now, and has been for the past ten years – so that in a sense I have come full circle, back to Bir Hassan, after many peregrinations.

Meanwhile I took my horses – still with Bijou among them – to join my friend Habib Cassir, who was the director of the Eperon Club, which was based at the City Sportive. Habib was married to a German girl, and was a great fan of all things German; but he was also extremely eccentric, and this led him to name all his horses after top Nazis. His own mare, a beautiful horse, he called Eva Braun. When he entered competitions with her, he would behave with a complete lack of inhibition if he didn't do well. If she refused a jump, or they kicked over a pole, he was not above dismounting, stamping the ground with rage, hurling his hat at the umpire, and stalking off, leaving Eva to be caught and led off by the stable boys. But for all that he was a kind man, and easy to get on with. I spent many long and happy years associated with the Eperon Club, while we continued to live at the villa at Bir Hassan.

By the beginning of the seventies, however, with the great influx of Palestinians and the swelling of the refugee camps, especially those of Sabra and Chatila nearby, it became clear that Bir Hassan was no longer a particularly safe place to stay. The Arabian Horse Club continued, but its membership began to fall off, leaving only a handful of loyal or especially keen riders to keep it going. Impending war brought about a stubbornness in people to maintain the normality of their lives as far as possible.

Jackie and I decided to move out, and we found another villa at a development in Mechref, outside Beirut but not too far to the south – Lebanon is a very small country – near Damour. By this time, Jackie had stopped flying, but I still had a commitment to the Eperon Club which entailed my being there for five and a half days a week. It was decided that Jackie would move out to Mechref, and I would rent a flat in Beirut where I would stay during the week, driving down to rejoin Jackie at weekends. The flat I found was the one in Raouche where I live now, though later, when Jackie rejoined me in Beirut, we were able to rent the adjacent apartment and knock them together, making one larger place. There was, however, to be a short intervening period when we were both in Mechref.

One morning in 1973 I arrived at the Eperon to find Habib in a great state of tension. Wandering from box to box in the stable yard were several armed Palestinian guerrillas. It looked as if they were sizing up the horses.

'What are they doing?' I asked Habib, filled with a sense of impending danger.

'I don't know, but something bad is about to start happening here,' he replied. 'I am going to move my horses out as soon as possible.' Habib owned a large hotel in the country, at Sofar, but the stabling there would not be sufficient for his and my horses together. I started to make enquiries about stables in Mechref, and eventually I managed to secure some. But I was just too late.

I will never forget the morning I arrived at the Eperon Club to be greeted by a bloodbath. Despite having seen and survived many other horrors since, this, being the first, was the most devastating, and remains so in my memory. Bijou and six other horses had been deliberately shot dead with rifles in their boxes. They lay in their own blood on the floor. Blood was flowing from their heads and necks across the floors of the boxes into the sand outside. I went behind the stables and was sick.

The horror was compounded by practical considerations – there was the difficult business of engaging carters to take the bodies away. I never discovered the reason why the horses had been killed. We couldn't talk to Palestinians in those days – we were terrified of them. I wouldn't have dared say, 'Why have you shot my horses?' They would have shot me. I believe they did it simply because they were owned by foreigners and were therefore foreign horses. I can imagine those fanatics simply saying to each other, 'Let's kill them all!' There was no other reason.

For the first time, the sense of isolation started which has persisted ever since; and we were all frightened. Things quickly became so tense that one dared not make even the most mildly contentious comment to one's best friend. As for the civil police, they had never been exactly efficient; now, what little authority they had collapsed completely, and they barely pretended to do their job. Palestinians would emerge from the camps to steal cars, forage for food, snatch purses. It was a bad time, when they were in the ascendant in Lebanon. The Lebanese were terrified of them, and slowly but surely they were taking over the country. Even so, Jackie and I never thought about leaving and returning to England. I suppose that after nearly thirty years there, we were becoming a bit like the Lebanese ourselves. They always said, *bukhra insh'allah hallas* – tomorrow, Allah will sort things out. Everyone stayed. The schools were still open – just. It was as if by pretending that everything was OK, everything *would* be OK. Meanwhile the Palestinians founded a huge unofficial city of their own – it was known as Arafat Land – behind the City Sportive. Yasser Arafat held court there, and they had their own prison, and their own tribunals and court-rooms. They were trying to set up a mini-state in Lebanon, a cuckoo in the nest. At the time of the Israeli invasion, the City Sportive and with it Arafat Land were destroyed.

Not all the horses had been killed. Four of mine had survived, and another five belonging to a North American called Tom Weaver; as there was stabling at Mechref, Tom and I decided, with the help of a couple of loyal truck drivers, to transport the remaining nine animals down there. Because of the heavy, and extremely touchy, Palestinian presence, this operation had to be performed secretly.

We chose a moonless night, went down to the club, and muffled the horses' hooves with sacking. It was fortunate that they knew us well and were not panicked by this unusual treatment, for the slightest loud noise from them and we would all have been dead. Though I was unarmed at the time, Tom had a pistol, and was quite prepared to use it. We moved the horses from the stables to where the trucks were waiting, a safe half mile down the road, two at a time, each of us leading one. It was a nerve-racking experience, and we had to keep an eye out for Palestinian sentries, who were posted all around with automatic rifles, and would certainly have shot on sight. When we reached the lorries, as we had no ramps to lead the horses up to the level of the platforms, the drivers had to back towards a small hillock, and we loaded the horses that way. We were both terrified throughout the five trips to and fro that we made, and I could never do such a thing again. Our main fear was that the horses already loaded would hear us coming with the others and start to neigh – or that they would pick up our nervousness and stamp their feet. Half a mile in the still of the night is not a great distance for sound to travel, and the Palestinians would have been upon us like a flash.

But we succeeded, and got all the animals safely to Mechref. I had not given up the flat in Beirut, but now I rejoined Jackie, and for several months our lives resumed a more even tenor. Tom Weaver, besides being a good horseman, was a teacher of English at the International College, which is an American college in Lebanon for junior students, and he used to bring children aged between about ten and fifteen down from there to ride at the little club we established around the stables at Mechref.

I was helped by a dear Danish friend of mine called Suzy, and her fiancé, Pierre Asseley, son of one of the leading families of Lebanon. There was no question of major showjumping competitions any more – the war had taken care of that – we had to concentrate on training the children to ride, together with some adult beginners. In the summers we took about twenty children on a two-week riding holiday in the mountains, staying at a beautiful farm which belonged to the head of Trans-Mediterranean Airlines, Munir Abu Heider, a keen rider himself, whose children trained with me.

Things went well for two years, and Jackie built up a splendid garden. Then, fighting broke out between the Amal Militia, Nabih Berri's men, and the Druze under Walid Jumblatt. Jumblatt was based up in Shemlan at first, but as time passed, the Druze began to filter down from the mountains, and the trouble started.

The man who had built the development at Mechref in which we lived was called George Debbas. He had been clever enough to identify the need for dwellings outside Beirut, and provided a full purchase service, including mortgage facilities. Several pilots from MEA lived there, former colleagues of Jackie among them. George was vigorously pro-Amal himself. He lived with his three sons in a magnificent villa in the middle of the estate he had constructed.

One night, Jackie and I were having supper at around eight in the evening when we heard shooting. It wasn't especially loud and we paid it no particular attention at first; everybody had his own gun, and people frequently used to practise on shooting ranges, or just fire exuberantly into the air. But when after fifteen minutes it was still going on, Jackie said, 'That's a little odd, isn't it?'

We got up from the table and went out on to the terrace.

Our villa was higher up the mountain than George's, and as we looked down on it, we saw that it was on fire.

'What's going on?' muttered Jackie.

'It's George's place – but he can't be under attack, surely? Not with all his bodyguards . . .'. We watched for a minute or so longer, scarcely able to believe what we saw. Then Jackie said, 'I'm going down.'

'Right; I'm coming too!'

We got the car out and drove down. As we drew level with George's front gate, we could see men in balaclavas with machine-guns in their hands running around the house, in the light of the flames.

'Christ,' said Jackie, 'let's get out of here – fast.'

We turned the car and drove quickly back up the hill again. Once home, I rang one of the MEA pilots. He was in a state of high excitement.

'Have you seen what's happening to George's house?' I asked.

'Yes – and for God's sake don't go anywhere near it. They've killed him and two of the boys – Henri and Sam.'

'What's happened to Roy?'

'As far as we know he got away. Hang on, I'll come round.'

He joined us, and we sat around together unable to do anything except watch as the fire consumed the house. Finally, after two hours, the flames died down, and there appeared to be no sign of any further movement around the house. We drove down, and Jackie and the pilot cautiously entered the house. Jackie told me afterwards that there were signs of the carnage everywhere, and the three bodies lay in the ruins. There was no trace of anyone else – neither militia nor George's bodyguards.

That was enough for us, and all the other expatriates at Mechref.

Jackie and I moved back to Beirut, and the flat in Raouche. Meanwhile, the horses had to be found a new home. I located one on the coast at Khalde, at the riding club owned and run by

Nhaar Najem and his Austrian wife, Eva. Nhaar's family had a bottling plant where they produced a local brand of orangeade. They were immensely rich, but Nhaar was a black sheep, and would not join the family business. He lived for riding, and for a time had been a trainer at the City Sportive for Fawzi Ghandour, the director of the Lebanese Equestrian Association. I found a haven here for a time, but the respite was to last no more than another year. When the Druze moved into Khalde in the course of their running battle with the pro-Syrian Amal, they simply moved into the club one day and annexed it, lock, stock and barrel, as their district operational headquarters. Nhaar told me that he had arrived at the club on Monday afternoon – the day when riding clubs are customarily closed – to find the Druze already in position, with tanks and guns lined up. When he asked what was happening, he was simply told to bugger off. We both lost all our stock – and he lost his property as well.

Back in Beirut, Jackie, bored with having no real gardening to do, was deep in plans to start a pub with a Lebanese friend called Munir Samaha, with whom we have since lost touch. They decided to call it the Pickwick Bar, and Jackie grew Victorian side-whiskers to go with the image: with his gold-rimmed half-moon spectacles he really looked the part. The pub was successful, and became *the* place in Beirut for all the remaining expatriates to meet. Jackie was kept very busy. He would get home from the lunchtime session at about three, and have a couple of hours' sleep before returning for the evening fray; but he enjoyed the Pickwick Bar.

The era of the car-bombs was approaching, and I was always nervous of his driving home late at night – you never knew when a parked car would explode and blow you to heaven or hell; but he laughed off my worries at that time, and also scoffed at my later fears of hostage kidnapping. 'Who would want an old man like me?' he used to ask. I remember him saying something to that effect not a month before he was taken.

Generally, life in Beirut in the late seventies and early eighties was getting increasingly difficult. I sought out the Arabian

Horse Club, to find it virtually at a standstill, though my old groom, Abu Ali, was still there. A bare handful of horses remained in the boxes, one of them an Irish mare which belonged to a Lebanese friend of mine called Claudette Hyek. Claudette asked me if I had the courage to go down to Bir Hassan and exercise the mare, and I agreed without thinking twice. I was only too glad to get on a horse again; and once I was back in the saddle, there was no stopping me. I simply could not live without horses.

It is interesting that it was horses that finally brought my daughter and me closer together. Jennifer took a job at Newmarket in her late teens as a stable groom, and the fact that she is mad on horses too has created a great bond between us now. Sadly, Jennifer's career took a severe setback when a two-year-old she was riding suddenly stood up on its hind legs and lost its balance, coming down on her and crushing one of her legs so badly that she was in and out of hospital for two years. It was during that time that I really got to know her. In happier days she was able to come out to Lebanon for a holiday with my grandchildren: Amanda is in her twenties now, and lives in Canada; Chris is with the RAF in Germany; Natasha is a keen member of the Pony Club, and lives with her mother.

At that time Kamal was still running the Arabian Horse Club, but Leonie had already returned to Sweden and they needed someone else to help out. I didn't need to be asked twice. Abu Ali was delighted. 'Why don't you try and find two or three new horses, Madam?' he suggested. 'I am sure that we could encourage people to come back and ride, now that you are here again.'

I took his advice and without much difficulty tracked down two nice horses which had been abandoned by owners who had fled. The Bedouin traders who had picked them up drove a hard bargain, but I still thought their acquisition was cheap at the price. They were called Emir, who cost LL150, and Bambi, who cost LL1300 being a mare; with them, the fortunes of the club began to pick up once again. Abu Ali and I nursed the new horses back into a state of good health – their vendors had not overfed them – and I went the rounds of my remaining acquaintances in Beirut, cajoling and persuading them to ride, telling them that it was not half as dangerous as they supposed. Nowadays, I laugh when I think of it. To get to the club today, I have to drive via Ouzai or the City Sportive. Ouzai is where much of the kidnapping has taken place, and much of the shelling is concentrated around the City Sportive, so I haven't a great choice.

I managed to get two or three people to come out; but once they started, they got back into the habit, and they began to bring their children. Chafika, the daughter of our old friend Selim Salaam, came along, and is still riding with us today. Another very talented young rider was Munir Awada. He had never ridden before, but from the minute he first sat on a horse I knew he was going to be outstanding. He had absolutely no fear, and was quite prepared to work every day and ride for an hour and a half, because he wanted to be the best. Sadly, after four months with us, his parents decided to send him away from Beirut; but he now owns two horses in Ireland and one in England, and he has entered competitions in both countries, and came third in one of them. Not bad at all! I am very proud of him.

As for Emir and Bambi, they survived the Israeli invasion, but were killed in the crossfire during a terrific battle which took place two years ago between the Amal and the Hezbollah militias.

About seven years ago, I bought a five-year-old mare from a farm over in the Bekaa Valley. She had been used as a farm horse, pulling some kind of rig, and you can still see the marks on her body where the harness rubbed. I noticed immediately that she became very nervous at the sight of a whip. She would put her ears back and retreat – obviously she'd had her share of beatings. I christened her Bijou II and quickly became very fond of her, because once she had relaxed she allowed her character to come out – and there was a lot of it. As she is a small horse, I'd bought her mainly for the children to ride, and they all love to give her a sugarlump or a carrot. Bijou II is clever; she learned very quickly how to ensure that she got her treats. Unless she got her carrot or sugarlump before the child got on her back, she wouldn't budge. She had regained so much confidence, too, that nothing would move her. I could shout and pull and push to my heart's content – but to no avail; the little rider might plead, kick, tug the reins – but equally in vain. Only a treat will get her moving.

Lately, Bijou II has refined her trick. When you take a child or a beginner round, you have the horse on the end of a longe – a training rein. You stand in the middle of the ring with the other end of the longe in one hand and a whip in the other. Bijou starts to go round perfectly well, but after eight or nine rounds she will start to slow up, and even a crack of the whip behind her won't make her speed up again. At the tenth round, she stops, and won't go on unless she is given some more sugar. It has happened often enough now for us to have established that it is consistently on the tenth round that she stops. The kids think it hilarious.

At the club, at the time of writing, we charge LL2,500 for half an hour, but everything is reckoned in US dollars now, because inflation is so grotesquely high that the Lebanese pound is in virtual abeyance. When I first had horses at the City Sportive, a load of feed cost about LL150; the same amount today would cost LL30,000. We use alfafa grass, as there is no hay here, and barley when we can get it, and chaff. For the boxes we use *inshara* – woodshavings from the local cabinetmakers and carpenters' shops. During the Israeli invasion and on occasion since, the craftsmen have closed their shops and we have had to use sand instead. Watering them is not a problem, as the club has its own well, which in these days is protected by a heavy, padlocked lid.

As far as the safety of the horses is concerned, the ones we have at present have just been lucky so far, as there is nothing we can do to protect them other than pray. We haven't always been fortunate.

We very rarely go for promenades along the sands any more. The beaches are controlled by the Amal, and there are checkpoints everywhere. Occasionally we go halfway to the airport, but it's a depressing outing, when you always have to take your identity card with you.

In 1981, a delightful family presented themselves at the club one day. Our meeting marked the start of what is now my most precious friendship. Amine Daouk is the son of an old Lebanese family, and although by training and profession he is an architect, he also owns substantial amounts of real estate – though he jokes that few people are interested in land purchase in Lebanon just at present. He is also on the board of several charities. Without him, it is no exaggeration to say that I would not have survived this long, or have written this book.

He arrived at the club that morning with his English wife, Kay, and their three daughters, Zein, Sarah and Soraya. At the time, the girls were twelve, ten and seven respectively. Sarah and Soraya still ride with me, and Amine is the supporting pillar of the club. As we stand now, we have thirty-eight horses and riders – which is not bad for a business in such an embattled position.

I would never have thought that Amine would turn into the rider he is today. After his daughters had been with me for a while, he decided that he would like to learn too; but it is not easy to start when you are over thirty, especially if you have never been on a horse before. Nevertheless, Amine was enthusiastic, and he persevered. I took him on a longe for the first two or three times, and he bounced happily round the circuit. He had been riding Emir, and, at his request, I took him off the longe and watched him bounce around the circuit, again quite happily, ten times. He kept his balance well, but he was not in rhythm with the horse at all, and I could see that Emir was getting fed up. Finally the horse simply stopped. Amine could not understand why, and gently kicked and pushed and encouraged – but to no effect. When Emir finally decided to move again, it was to walk wearily towards the stable, where I stood.

'What's the matter with him?' asked Amine.

'He doesn't want you to break his back,' I grinned, and explained what was going wrong. Amine smiled back ruefully, and dismounted – but as soon as his feet touched the ground, he collapsed.

'My legs don't seem to want to hold me up,' he said apologetically. I told him not to worry – he had suffered the usual fate of beginners, who cling too tightly with their leg muscles to the sides of the horse. Amine recovered, and persevered.

Sarah and Soraya were riding quite well on their own by that time, Sarah on a delightful little dun mare from the mountains, with the most gentle and affectionate nature, called Bambina. Soon, Amine was trotting around the ring after them, and it was not long before he wanted to join us on a promenade. I was not sure that he was absolutely ready, but I decided to mount him on Emir again, as the horse had a very long-suffering nature.

All went well to start with, but then the other horses began to canter. Emir followed suit, with Amine hanging on for all he was worth. Then Emir spotted a lovely patch of lush grass, and decided to head for it. The others had not noticed, and rode on. There was nothing Amine could do to make Emir change his mind – as Emir well knew. He made a beeline for the grass, reached it, and abruptly stopped. Poor Amine, however, went on. He sailed straight over Emir's head and landed flat on his back. By the time he had managed to collect himself, Emir had seen the other horses coming back, so he galloped off to join them, bringing up the rear and heading for the stables with them, leaving Amine to walk the two miles in riding boots, on tottery legs, on a stinking hot day. He arrived eventually, and I asked him rather nervously whether after that experience he still wanted to go on riding. Being the sportsman he is, there was only one reply:

'Certainly!'

7

DOGS OF WAR

Animals have always played a central role in my life, and if horses have been my ruling passion, dogs have run them a very close second. I have always had a dog, since the age of three. Almost as soon as we arrived in Lebanon, we began to acquire strays. There were always dozens of them on the dunes – abandoned house dogs and their offspring, but usually gentle, and longing for affection. The Koran teaches that dogs are unclean. Mehdi, my Lebanese friend who is a cameraman for Independent Television News in London, is as fearless a man as you could hope to meet; yet he treats my toy poodle with the utmost caution.

Nowadays, sophisticated and cosmopolitan Lebanese do have pet dogs, but that was rarely the case in the fifties. The president, Camille Chamoun, owned dogs, but they were for hunting – working animals, not pets. I remember that Jackie had a cartoon-like encounter with the local dog-catchers, who used to drive around in a van with a trap door in its top. Seated on the back was a man with a long pole that ended in a wire noose. He'd snatch up unattended dogs on the street with this, and drop them into the van through the trap door. One day at Bir Hassan they took one of our 'family', a motley terrier called Rover, but they weren't quick enough for Jackie not to notice and attempt a rescue. I got home from riding to find Jackie perched on the roof of the van holding Rover, engaged in a tug-of-war with the dog-catcher at the other end of the noose-and-pole. I fetched a big stick and joined in the fray, hitting the man, who eventually released the noose so that Jackie could slip it over Rover's head; but then the van driver suddenly drove away, so that Jackie and Rover overbalanced and fell to the ground, fortunately only getting a few minor bruises as a result.

An unpleasant experience I had early on in Lebanon would have been a good deal worse if it had not been for one of our 'unofficial' dogs. At that time the dunes around Beirut were clean and empty, just like the desert, and I had a favourite walk which led towards the little wood I mentioned earlier which the army had turned into an assault-course. One day I was walking there with a motley entourage of dogs, including a little orange terrier called Max; all dogs are called Max in Lebanon, by the way, and all bitches, Stella. Max was particularly fond of me, for some reason. They had run on ahead when someone came up behind me silently and grabbed me by the neck.

'If you scream I'll put a knife in you,' he said, tightening his grip. I remember the words exactly. He pulled me down on to the sand and started to undo my slacks; they were tight-fitting with a complicated buttoning arrangement, which gave him trouble. Nevertheless, he managed to pull them half off, and then removed a hand from my mouth in order to undo his own trousers. Immediately, I yelled for Max. The man didn't pay any attention. He simply grinned. By now he had his trousers down, and I started to panic as he lowered himself on top of me; but before he could go any further, Max came tearing up, and bit the man smartly in the leg. He yelled and let go of me immediately, turning to pay attention to his wound, for Lebanese, not without reason, are terrified of rabies. It took me a split second to pull my slacks up and start running, shouting to Max to follow me. I made for the wood, where by the grace of God there were some soldiers. They searched for the man, but he had made himself scarce by then.

After all this time, I am still frightened when someone walks too close behind me in the street, and I feel deep sympathy for all rape and attempted rape victims. I do not believe that even the most sensitive men can have more than an inkling of the damage such an experience can do.

The two dogs which dominated the middle period of our lives in Lebanon were Simba and Husky. Simba was part mountain dog, and belonged entirely to Jackie. He loved Jackie so jealously, in fact, that if even I came too close to him, Simba would snarl. He and Husky were mortal enemies, as Husky loved me almost as fiercely as Simba loved Jackie, though Husky was overall a more intelligent and gentle dog. The enmity between them had a marked effect on our lives, and as they were more or less exact contemporaries, and lived long lives, the sacrifices we made on their behalf were considerable.

We had rescued Simba's mother, Karima, when her owners, our neighbours when we were living in the villa at Bir Hassan, threw her out on discovering that she was pregnant. Most sadly, she died while giving birth to Simba, her only puppy, whom Jackie hand-reared. No wonder Simba adored him.

Husky's mother was Snowflake, a husky who belonged to an American couple who had acquired her while filming sled-dogs in the Arctic. She was pregnant too when they were in Lebanon, and Husky was the first dog of his breed to be born there. He was my constant companion from 1968 to 1980, when he died of thrombosis. In his time, he became a celebrity in Lebanon.

Whenever the dogs came together, they fought. We solved this when Jackie lived at Mechref by the simple expedient of locking Simba in Jackie's bedroom when I came down for the weekend with Husky. When we all moved back to Beirut permanently, the only original point of contact between the two flats which were to become one was via the balconies, so that the dogs could be shut away from it. But it was an inconvenience we got used to, and finally did not notice.

Jackie left Middle East Airlines in about 1960 under unfortunate circumstances. Although normally he has a very gentle nature, he can flare up suddenly, and he is very proud. I think he had been frustrated at work for some time by the intricacies of Levantine office politics, and at a cocktail party one day it all came to a head. The fact that he had had a couple of drinks too many did not help, but the long and the short of it was that he had a row with the then managing director and told him what he could do with his job. Everyone was very distressed, and the whole matter might have blown over in a couple of days, but unfortunately Jackie would neither apologise nor retract what he had said. As he had been with MEA for so long, rather than sack him, they suggested that he offer his resignation, which would be accepted. And so that was the end of his flying. Of course there was no pension.

For a while thereafter, Jackie ran boarding kennels from our villa in Bir Hassan. There were enough expatriate pet-owners who would lodge their dogs with us when they went home on leave to keep him busy, and at one time we had over twenty dogs to feed, counting our own strays. It was quite a thing to see all the dishes laid out on the large kitchen table: boarders were fed first, and strays second. One boarder I particularly remember was called Donald. He was a Golden Cocker spaniel who arrived one day in a large chauffeur-driven car complete with his own basket, special day- and night-coats, as well as toys and brushes galore. The chauffeur informed us that Donald must not have too much exercise in case he became tired, and must wear his coat at all times. After two days, however, Donald was running free and coatless with the rest of the pack, and having the time of his life. I was sorry to see him go back to his gilded cage.

The kennels did not last long – no more than a year – for Jackie found that his heart was not in running them. He took a job with the administrative staff at Trans-Mediterranean Airlines. That lasted for several years, until history repeated itself and he tore the managing director off a strip, and resigned. This was embarrassing, as the managing director's children rode with me, but eventually we managed to paper over the cracks. Since then, Jackie has worked for himself. Fortunately, he is quite an astute investor, and has managed to triple our savings. The pensions we get from England are minuscule, since we have barely lived there. We have bank accounts in Jersey and London as well as Beirut, but at the moment I cannot touch them, as withdrawals require Jackie's signature. I am, therefore, in a bad way financially, despite help from various organisations and hostage-aid charities, and the rent on my flat has not been paid since Jackie disappeared. I am worried that the landlords will try to have me evicted.

One of the problems about moving away from Lebanon, however, is that while we can live comfortably here, it is only because the rents are so low. We would find it expensive in Cyprus, and impossibly dear in England.

We were still at Bir Hassan when someone gave Jackie a little gazelle, whom we christened Gaston. As a companion for him, we acquired a nanny goat, called Miranda, and the two of them lived in a wire enclosure in the garden. Husky befriended Gaston, and always defended him against strange dogs – for although our animals were used to him, and treated him as one of the family, a dog's natural instinct would be to chase a gazelle and kill it. I remember the first morning I decided to let Gaston take part in one of our Sunday promenades. The day before, I explained to Husky what I had in mind, and told him that he should look after Gaston. Husky spent the rest of the day in Gaston's pen, explaining to him. Then the next morning, the two of them set off together as if by arrangement, long before the horses had even started. Miranda the goat brought up the rear. She could never keep up and used to bleat furiously at us before giving up and stumping back to the villa alone – there to await Gaston's return and give him a sharp piece of her mind.

The autumn and winter of 1968, when Husky was four

months old, were the worst experienced in Lebanon for twenty-two years. The rain came down in torrents, and there was a flood. The water came over the tops of our gumboots, and horses stood up to their hocks on soggy *inshara*. We tried pumping some of the water out of the boxes – unfortunately, all of them were occupied at the time, so we could not move the horses to empty boxes while we tried to drain their own – but with very little success. We also had plenty of trouble with our domestic animals. Gaston and Miranda had a sleeping pen by the side of the house, which we thought was on high enough ground to stay dry, and Husky was inside the house. However, one morning I got up to find Husky outside, swimming desperately to try to get back. He must have gone out to check up on his friends and fallen into the flood water which had covered most of the garden. The wind and the continuing downpour made matters worse, and Husky looked as if he were in danger of being swept away, as if by a tide. I only had a sweater and slacks on, not even shoes, but I plunged into the icy water to rescue him. He was very wet and frightened. I parked him in the kitchen and went round to check on Gaston and Miranda, who, I discovered, had also been flooded out. Gaston was treading water and Miranda, who was much bigger, was standing up to her neck, bleating pathetically. I called to Abu Ali – my faithful groom who later joined the Arabian Horse Club – to give me a hand. Miranda allowed herself to be rescued quite demurely, but poor little Gaston, who was normally a perfect gentleman, was so petrified and miserable that he butted Abu Ali when he tried to pick him up, and knocked him headlong into the water. It was hysterical!

Eventually, we all got ourselves to the kitchen with the animals and stood in a dripping group in the middle of the floor. Later, I went up to the City Sportive and managed to beg some spare boxes for five of our horses. We walked them up in the teeming rain, rubbed them down and got them into their new, dry lodgings. As for our remaining twelve mounts, we took them out of their boxes and tethered them to a stake on some ground which was high enough to be above the flood, putting blankets on their backs. There they stood for two days, until the rain abated.

Among our other animals were Shadow and Pancho. Pancho was a grey African parrot whom I inherited from a seaman who was emigrating to Canada. Pancho loved television, and his favourite programme was 'Popeye'. When that came on, he would leap up and down on his perch, screaming abuse in the bluest of language. Pancho also loved to drive around in the car, but this could be risky, because he was given to hurling similar invective at other drivers.

We found Shadow out on the dunes. He was a pointer, but he had been shot in the hind legs and abandoned. He could not walk at all when we found him, and although with care he made a partial recovery, he was never able to move quickly. We called him Shadow because he attached himself to Husky and became his most devoted friend. In the car, Husky would always sit on the back seat behind the driver, and Shadow beside him, behind the front passenger seat. These were their invariable positions, just as Pancho would sit next to me, when we later made the weekly trip between Beirut and Mechref.

Soon after the troubles started I was driving back to the flat on a Monday morning when a sniper opened fire at the car. One shot hit Pancho, another, Shadow. Pancho died immediately, but Shadow was wounded and in agony. I drove hell for leather to a vet that I knew, but it was too late. Shadow was dead by the time I got there. If the sniper had been positioned on the other side of the road, his shots would have found Husky and myself.

Poor Husky was inconsolable, especially as only two weeks earlier he had lost Gaston, when an outsider dog broke into his enclosure at night and killed him. Gaston had been moved to Mechref, and when Husky arrived to find his friend gone, he lay down in the empty pen and gave himself up to grief. He refused food, and so deep was his sorrow that Jackie even suggested letting Simba loose, in the hope that a fight would bring Husky back to his old self. I was willing to try anything, but Husky merely looked at Simba sorrowfully, and Simba, failing to encounter any answering aggression, lost interest himself. As for Miranda, she pined for lack of company so much that we gave her to a local goat herd. She settled into his flock quite happily.

Husky was an intelligent dog, bred for work. In the early seventies, following fighting there, an appeal went out from the Shia leaders to help the destitute people of the south of the country, especially the children, and I decided to do something, enlisting Husky's aid. I got hold of a basket, and Jackie made a little cart to fit it to, with a light harness for Husky. With this, we went out and made a collection of presents for the children of the south. Husky's appeal, in a country where the people are not automatically well-disposed towards dogs, was as immediate as it was unexpected. Everyone took him to their hearts. That first public appearance culminated with an invitation to the Loup Garou night-club at the Federal Hotel on Christmas Eve, 1974. Husky went with Jackie, as I had flu, but the evening made a star out of the dog. Later in his career, he was even to receive Valentine's cards.

At the Loup Garou, as well as further donations for the children, Husky received a number of presents for himself, including a roast chicken, but these he shared with our strays, and it gave me the idea that if he could collect for children, why shouldn't he collect for stray dogs on the dunes as well? This he did later, with equal success. The strays are still with us, even today, and I try to take food to them at least three times a week. Someone has to look after them, and what else can you do, if you love animals? There has never been the equivalent of an RSPCA in Lebanon. I tried to form one, but with no success.

Husky was invited to make a guest appearance at Spinneys Centre on his seventh birthday. Spinneys was the biggest and best department store in Beirut, a short way from the City Sportive. Mr Sifri, the manager, presented him with a beautiful blanket for his basket, together with LL100 (a lot of money in those days) to buy food for the strays. Four days later, I happened to be passing Spinneys and saw that it was on fire. It had been set alight by the Palestinians, who were now ransacking it, though other looters were getting in on the act. The reason for this action was that the owner was English. A satisfying story arises from this misfortune: one of the looters had parked his large new Mercedes outside. He had already filled it with goods, but decided to dash back in for just one more haul. When he came out again, he found that someone else had stolen his car and driven off in it.

The highlight of Husky's career was when he became a model. When president Camille Chamoun's son, Danny, married for the first time, it was to an Australian model called Patti. She was about ten years older than he was, and he married her in London against his father's wishes. His father was furious, but Danny managed to get his mother on his side, so things were patched up and he brought Patti back to Beirut. A big party was arranged, according to Lebanese custom, for Patti to meet all her new relatives. It was a very sophisticated 'do'; but Patti was a down-to-earth Australian, and didn't give a damn about what anyone thought.

Everyone turned up to the reception in their finest clothes and jewellery – but Patti was nowhere to be seen. Finally she appeared, but dressed very informally, and accompanied by her mother, who was a real outback Australian. She had been Patti's dresser in her modelling days, and Patti took her everywhere. We all loved her and called her 'mum'; but she was too much for the Chamouns – she, and Patti's disrespectful dress. Patti looked round the roomful of frozen dignitaries and said, 'Don't worry, mum, it's perfectly all right – they're just ordinary people; there's no need to be shy.' And that was the end of it. She was never really accepted by the Chamoun family after that. The marriage survived, but not indefinitely.

Patti, who was never one to be put down by anybody, not only weathered the storm, but decided to stay in Lebanon and go into business for herself. She started a modelling agency. When the Chamouns learned that their daughter-in-law was in commerce, there was an uproar. But Patti quite simply didn't give a damn. Her agency was a terrific success and she made money hand over fist.

One day in mid-1975 we were chatting and she told me that she had a crisis on her hands. She was putting on a show at the huge and luxurious Phoenicia Hotel two nights later, but her top model had had to drop out because she had contracted measles, of all things.

'I'm stuck. I can't find an adequate replacement, and so I want to do something totally different. Got any ideas?'

'What about a horse? I could bring one down.'

She looked very doubtful, but then her face cleared. 'Wait a moment. What about your dog?'

'Husky?'

'Yeah. He pulls a basket around, doesn't he?'

'Yes.'

'Right. I'll get hold of a small kid who'll fit in the basket and we'll think of something for the two of them to do. Bring Husky round with his stuff tomorrow for a rehearsal. It'll be a sensation.'

It was my turn to be doubtful. 'Are you sure? You know they're not keen on dogs here.'

'Nonsense. It'll be great.'

In the event she was right. Husky opened and closed the show. He was walked by Tracey Chamoun, Patti's daughter, a teenager by then and embarking on her own modelling career. Husky pulled his basket, in which sat a little child dressed in the latest children's fashions and holding satin 'reins'. On the sides of the basket were pinned the names of the fashion shops from which the clothes could be obtained. Husky was paid LL50 – he had become a professional.

About this time, Husky gained a new friend. Sealy – so named because he looked like a baby seal – was a stray puppy which we found abandoned. At first Husky was snooty about him, though Sealy clearly loved Husky from day one. However, their friendship was confirmed after Husky rescued his little sidekick from an attack by a strange dog during a walk one day.

One of their first adventures together was up at Ferayah in the winter. Neither of them had ever seen snow before, but Husky took to it naturally. Sealy, however, was a Lebanese pie-dog through and through, and deeply mistrustful of it. The children who were with us decided that they would make little chamois boots for Sealy, and once he had them on, he overcame his misgivings and was soon romping in the snow as to the manner born.

On walks along the beach, they would compete to see which of them could catch the most sand-crabs. On one occasion a large crab pinched Sealy squarely on the nose. Sealy yelped and dashed over to Husky for comfort and protection; but Husky merely told him not to be so silly in future, and stick to catching smaller crabs.

Then they both went missing. Practically all the children in Beirut were in consternation, for Husky had become their hero. I had no idea what might have happened to them, but it seemed clear that, as no bodies had been found, they had been stolen. As Husky was not only a valuable dog, but a local hero, it seemed likely that he would be held to ransom. This was no comfort as we waited to hear from his supposed kidnappers. We were also fearful for Sealy, who was undistinguished and could quite easily have been killed; but in this at least our fears were soon assuaged because a neighbour of ours found him on the sand dunes a couple of days later. He was frightened, filthy and hungry, and very pleased to be home.

I was sure Sealy would not have strayed far from where Husky and he had been parted, which gave me the vaguest of clues about Husky's whereabouts. I was wondering what to do about it when help came from an unexpected quarter.

A little girl telephoned me to see if there was any news of Husky. When I told her that there was none, she said she would ask her father, who was a captain in the army, to look for him on my behalf. I didn't take her seriously but thanked her anyway, and I was very surprised when the following day a sergeant and half a dozen soldiers arrived at the flat to tell me that they had been deputed to search for Husky. I told them where I thought he might be, and they combed the area, but without success. I then asked if I could join them. At first they were reluctant because they feared it could be dangerous, but finally they relented, and I went with them, calling Husky's name loudly. We had almost given up hope when, at last, we heard a faint answering bark.

It came from a tumbledown building, which the soldiers broke into, surprising two men inside. The captain, who had come with us, went with me into a basement room where Husky was chained to a stake so tightly that his neck was bruised and bleeding. We quickly unlocked the chain and Husky sprang into my arms with such enthusiasm that he knocked me flying. The kidnappers said that they had found Husky wandering on the dunes and were keeping him until they could locate his rightful owner, but this thin story did not prevent the soldiers from beating them up. I did not prefer charges, partly because of their beating, but mainly because I was too pleased and relieved to see Husky again to bother with anything else. Sealy was, if anything, even happier than me. He didn't leave Husky's side for three days. As for the captain's little girl, Husky sent her a photo of himself signed with his pawmark on the back, and she and her father came round for tea and cakes, and for her to give Husky a kiss.

Sealy did not survive Husky long. His death, at seven years old, was accidental and sad. At that time a Romanian lady called Mme Stefan ran a beauty salon for dogs, and I would take Sealy there for a shampoo, and to be de-flea'd. Normally everything went well, but this time Mme Stefan used a new type of flea-toxin which, though in solution, proved to be too strong. It poisoned Sealy through the pores of his skin, and despite being rushed to a vet, it was too late to save him, and I had to have him put down. Mme Stefan was as upset as I was – Sealy had been going to her for years and had always had the best possible treatment. As she had pet poodles herself, she promised me the next puppy that came along, if I would like one.

Simba had also died, and been replaced with a curious looking stray called Tinkerbell by Jackie – TB for short. He was a long-haired terrier-sized mixture, but once Mme Stefan had given him a trim, he emerged as a dog which you could describe as eighty per cent Schnauzer. He adored Jackie, but nothing would induce Jackie to walk him, so I had to. TB's great joy in life was to get hold of an empty carton, stick his head in it, and rampage round the flat – flying blind. All you could see was a cardboard box on legs.

All was well until I left for my annual holiday in England. I stressed to Jackie the importance of walking TB on a lead, because of his wild ways and because of the uncaring Lebanese traffic, but he only gave me half-promises. Simba had never been on a lead – why should TB need one? While I was away he ignored my warnings, and the result was that poor TB was run over and killed. Jackie was terribly upset, and cabled me in England that I should buy a poodle to bring back, as Mme Stefan's bitch showed no signs of being in pup. In fact, I had already been thinking along similar lines, but I had left it too late, and was now due to return.

Our next dog, Zara, did come from Mme Stefan. She was a lovely, fresh, gay little thing, and confirmed my liking for poodles; but she, too, was killed by a reckless driver in a hit-and-run accident which also left me with a permanently damaged leg. I was desolate, as I cannot live without a dog. I decided to see if there was any chance of obtaining another poodle in West Beirut. None was to be had; the only pet shop, Puppies' Garden, had reopened after the Israeli invasion, but still had little stock. Their animals had normally come from England or France, and as the airport was closed, nothing was arriving. All they had were some Siamese kittens. The owner, whom I know well, said, 'Why don't you take one of them?

They're half-dog anyway, and as you're so unhappy, it would be much better than nothing.' I weakened and chose one. She was adorable, with big impertinent blue eyes and little black ears that stood straight up.

I took her home and Jackie fell for her immediately. We christened her Sasha. She wasn't much older before she started the territorial war with Jackie over his balcony-gardens, despite the fact that she had two large flowerpots filled with sand for her personal use. It is a war that is still going on.

Eight months passed, and there was still no sign of an available poodle, so I bought a light collar and lead for Sasha and took her out for walks. She was quite happy with this arrangement but we drew some curious looks and comments.

'Cat,' people would observe.

'Yes, cat,' I would reply.

Then I heard that Puppies' Garden had acquired some poodle puppies from the East Side, and I went down to Manara to see them. All but one had been sold, and the solitary leftover was in a sorry state. She was the runt, she had canker in both ears, her tail had not been docked, although she was already nearly a year old, and she had a liver complaint which swelled her up like a balloon.

'Are you sure this is the only one?' I asked.

Then she looked at me. Tara has hazel eyes, which I have never seen in a dog before – they are normally grey, brown or blue; but her eyes are like lamps. I returned her gaze. We understood one another immediately.

'I'll take her,' I said. She took some cleaning up, and we had to get her tail done, but I have never regretted my decision. It crossed my mind that we might have a problem with Sasha, but the two of them got on well from the very beginning, and now they are the greatest of friends. They play tag around the flat. First of all Sasha leads and goes off at full tilt in and out of the bedrooms, through the salon, and then back through the kitchen and across the balconies, with Tara in hot pursuit; then they change round and Tara is 'it', and so it goes on until they are both exhausted. I prefer animals to humans; an animal is dependent on you when it's ill; it's always grateful, and it never answers back. Above all, they give you so much love. Any animal does – dog, cat or horse. That's why I've always adored them.

I should not conclude this chapter without mentioning another Max. He is a blind dog who lives not far from my flat; he is blind because he was hit by shrapnel, but he gets along well enough, because the Koran teaches that you must succour the afflicted, and the local children look after him. I met him first in August 1989. The weather was at its hottest. I was walking Tara, and to find some shade we crossed the road by a squat inhabited by Lebanese refugees from the south who have been there ever since the Israelis pushed them out of their homes in 1982. Something took Tara's attention and she wandered off – as there were no cars around, I wasn't too perturbed. I saw her stop, and her tail begin to wag; then she looked back at me and I called to her. She barked back that I should come over, which I did, and found her nose to nose with Max, having a chat. He is a long, brown-haired mongrel, about the size of a terrier, and about two years old. There is no indication that he is blind. The local children came up and told me that. He lives in a compound next to where the refugees live, and they leave the door that leads to the stairwell of their building open so that he can shelter there if ever it rains. Still, they don't have much food to give him, so now I go down two or three times a week and fill him up.

8

MY KIDNAP

I have a blue glass bead in the form of an eye. Most Muslims carry one, and its purpose is to ward off the Evil Eye – to keep you out of trouble. I have had it now for fifteen years, and I have never taken it off, although once I nearly lost it, when I was driving. A gunman waved me down, and when I stopped he leant into the car and said, 'I want your gold chain.' He snatched it from my neck before I could reply, snapping the clasp. The blue bead was attached to it and fell into the gutter, but I retrieved it. It is the only jewellery I wear now – rings or bracelets would be taken from me. I replaced the gold chain with a silver one, but as soon as I have any money, the first thing I will buy is a new gold chain for it. It has taken me through every adventure I have had in Lebanon since the war started, and so far it has kept me from death.

It was given to me when the wars started, shortly after the horses were killed at the Eperon Club, by a captain in the Lebanese army who rode with me, and who had fallen in love with me. He wanted me to leave Jackie and marry him. Of course, nothing came of it, but he told me that as I would not accept a ring, he wanted to give me an Arab blessing, so that I would be safe. When he gave me the bead he told me never to go anywhere without it, as that way I would never come to harm.

I had the bead when I was kidnapped myself. I was driving home from the City Sportive with Husky when a car suddenly pulled in in front of me and forced me on to the kerb. Another vehicle pulled up behind me. Several men with guns emerged from either car, and tried to force me out, but after Husky had bitten one of them on the arm, they decided that it would be easier to make me follow the first car, with the second bringing up the rear. We drove into Arafat Land and stopped. I was told to get out of my car, and I did so, but only on condition that Husky could stay with me. I didn't know what it was all about, of course, but I learned later that one of the PLO's top men had been blown up by a car-bomb on Verdun Street that morning, and someone had seen a foreign blonde woman walking away from the scene, who seemed to be implicated in the murder.

They put me through five hours of interrogation, at the end of which I was almost incoherent with nerves. They asked me who I was, where I'd been that day, how long I'd been in Lebanon. I'd been there longer than any of them, longer than some of them had been alive. When I told them I'd spent the morning at the riding club, they looked very displeased. 'You've been riding horses while our great leader was being assassinated,' they accused. I could hardly point out that I hadn't known that their great leader was going to be assassinated at precisely that time, so I said that I was very sorry, but that it really had nothing to do with me. It transpired from what they said that the foreign blonde had hired a car on the East Side and parked it, full of dynamite, outside the barber's where their man used to go every morning for a massage. As they had picked me up on the Airport Road, they clearly thought I was making my getaway. I explained again that I had known nothing at all about it, but I was getting more and more frightened. Worst of all, the man whom Husky had bitten stood in the doorway, nursing a bloodily bandaged arm and glaring at Husky and me balefully. I knew he would kill both of us if he could.

By the grace of God they let me go. One of their leaders turned up, and he knew me from the riding school at Bir

Hassan – he had been our neighbour. He knew that there was no way that I could be connected with the assassination, and after a few clipped orders to them, and apologies to me, I was allowed to leave. It was several days, however, before I could bring myself to drive that way again.

When I got back to the flat, the experience suddenly hit me and I started to shake. Jackie was there, but he hadn't been worried – I hadn't been away long enough, I suppose. Then he saw me trembling.

'What's up with you?'

I could hardly get the words out: 'I've just been kidnapped!'

'What are you talking about? Don't be silly – you can't have been kidnapped – you're here!'

'Yes, but I've been away hours – didn't you miss me? Hadn't you noticed that I hadn't come back from the club at my usual time?'

'No,' he said. 'I just thought you were riding late.'

'Oh,' I said. 'Thank you – thank you very much!' Then I collapsed in tears. 'At least get me a brandy or something.'

Finally it dawned on him that I really was in a state. I told him the whole story, but once I'd finished all he said was, 'Well, there you are! I've told you and told you not to go out to that place all the time on your own. You've been asking for trouble.'

'Well, I got it today, didn't I?'

'I'll never be able to get any sense into your head.'

Jackie was like that – he could be very brusque, but immediately afterwards he would follow it up with some kind act or other – usually in the form of a present. His roughness covered real concern.

Not long after this I had another close shave – this time a militia man flagged the car down when Husky and I were driving home and told me to get out.

'What do you want?' I said, not budging.

He opened the passenger door and leaned in, waving a .45 automatic. 'I want your car, and your dog,' he announced.

I thought, you'd be welcome to the car, chum, but you're not having my dog. I swung my legs round on the seat and kicked him hard between the legs. While he was pre-occupied, I slammed the car into gear and roared off. When I got home, Jackie gave his usual offhand reaction, pointing out that if the gun had gone off, I'd have quite possibly been killed. I helped myself to a large gin and tonic and felt better. Normally, I only drink beer, but spirits are a great help *in extremis*.

As the war progressed, the incidence of kidnapping escalated. We thought we had had enough trouble in Beirut with everything we had already been through, but suddenly matters got worse than ever. 'They' started taking hostages – one always says 'they', because one never knows who exactly is responsible. People began to disappear in unbelievable ways. Once, they took four people at the same time, three Lebanese and one Indian, all teachers at the University of Beirut. By that time, they had already taken American hostages too; they were, though it is terrible to have to say it, the most popular targets. Later, they started on the English. It is difficult for me, now that my husband is a hostage, to say how I felt then. I suppose you never feel the full force of anything until it touches you personally. We used to say, 'My God, how awful; who's been taken now?' – and we'd all agree that Beirut was becoming worse and worse, and that no one was safe any more; then we'd get on with our shopping.

The first time kidnapping was really brought home to me – apart from my own brief taste of it – was in 1986 when the son of a great riding friend of mine was taken. His name was Omar Dhabbari, and his father kept his horse, Bourj, with me at the Arabian Club. The whole family were keen riders. Omar was a very charming young man – always in trouble with the family, but most likeable.

One day I arrived at the club and Adnan Alamuddine, one of the staunchest members of the club, who has been on hand through our darkest days, came up to me with a worried look on his face and said, 'Sunnie, have you heard the news? Omar's been taken.'

'Good God, no!'

'Yes; he was taken last night as he left the university – four men got him – bundled him into the boot of a car and drove off.'

That really hit me – more than news of any of the other hostages had, for I knew Omar well and liked him a lot; and all his family I counted as friends. I thought how awful it was for this happy, carefree young man to be taken off like that. As soon as I got home, I rang up his father to ask if there was anything I could do. He said no – he was working on it and hoped to have some news before too long. I told him to let me know as soon as there was any development, but heard no more for five days.

Then Mona Dhabbari rang me to say that the kidnappers had contacted him and demanded one million Lebanese pounds for the return of his son. The Dhabbaris were wealthy, but the sum demanded was still very large. They could not just go to the bank and draw out that amount.

'What's going to happen?' I asked.

'Well,' he replied, 'I've talked to various Syrians in charge of security in West Beirut, and the consensus is that we'll have to negotiate with the kidnappers.'

The kidnappers had allowed forty-eight hours for the money to be paid. If it was not, they had issued the usual threats; that is, they would begin by sending one of Omar's fingers to his father. . . . A rendez-vous was arranged, and a Syrian security man carried a bag to the 'drop' and left it there. But the bag contained no money, only a note to say that the sum demanded was too great. Half a million was offered instead, and, the note continued, if this was not accepted the Syrians would storm the house where Omar was being held. This last was a bluff, as no one had any idea where he was. However, the kidnappers contacted Mona shortly afterwards and told him that they would accept the half million. He paid, and Omar was released.

I did not see him until about a week later, because his father took him up into the mountains to rest. Omar was very subdued; a different person, in fact. He told me that he had been tied up and blindfolded throughout the week of his capture. He never said any more, nor did he tell who his kidnappers had been. He seemed to want to block out the entire episode. But the change in his personality hit me hard – I felt sorry for him, and tried to imagine what it must have been like, tied up in that basement. But it is frustrating – no matter what you think, no matter how *much* you think – you cannot *do* anything, because you do not know where the hostages are, or who is holding them. It is unbearable to have no word at all. One needs something to react to.

We all felt the same way about Terry Waite, on the West Side – that he would find himself in trouble. We knew he would be all right the first time he came over, as the Druze militia who were his bodyguards had been well paid. At the time of his kidnap the rumour in Beirut was that his guard just walked out and left him, but no reason was given. Maybe they didn't think they were getting enough money that time. Everybody was terribly sorry when he was taken because he was so well-known and seemed so brave; but then other stories started to circulate in Lebanese society – that he was not quite such a hero as he had seemed, that in a sense he had asked for it, by using the situation in Beirut as a means of boosting his own standing. It was even said that he was after a Nobel Prize. I don't know – I have never met him. People who have say that he is a charming man.

The news of his disappearance came out very slowly. On the wireless, they kept saying that nothing had been heard of Terry Waite, but that they were hoping to have some fresh information soon. Nobody in West Beirut was surprised, though Jackie was very upset, and spent his time glued to the wireless when the news was on. We were all hoping that it was not true that he had been kidnapped; but the fact brought the danger home to us for a while. People were frightened to go out. I was more afraid of them trying to take my car again, and perhaps taking me, not so much as a hostage, but to rape. I have heard of three such cases. They are quite prepared to do that kind of thing if they get the chance, and I am not flattering myself: any woman will do. The people we are dealing with are not normal: they are gangs of thugs with no feelings, or pride, or anything else. As far as a woman is concerned, her car is useful, but she is not – a woman is too difficult for them to keep as a hostage, so the system is to rape the driver and take the car.

I have mentioned the police force. Even in the old days of peace, they were never very forceful, and mainly directed the traffic. I don't think any policemen were promoted to do anything more than that. They certainly didn't come from the ranks of the educated Lebanese. You would never go to a policeman and tell him you had been robbed, for all he would say would be, *mafisha* – none of my business. You would have to go to see the head of security. I have also mentioned the fire service. But our ambulance service is still very good, run by both the International Red Cross and the Lebanese Red Crescent.

If you were taken ill at home, you would phone the family doctor, if the phones were working, and if he had not left for the USA or Canada. The telephones work rarely. We have had periods of months when they don't function, as lines are always down in one part of the city or another, and exchanges have not been immune from the shelling. I remember once when our telephone was out of order. We waited for ten days for something to happen and then I got fed up, and went over to the exchange to complain.

'What is your number?' the official asked me.

I told him, and he said, 'Then why are you here?'

'I'm here to tell you that my phone isn't working. It hasn't been working for ten days! That's not good enough!'

He looked at me. 'Ten days? Count yourself lucky. Most of the numbers with your prefix have been out for three months. We have two men on the repair crew and they will work their way round to you. In the meantime, go home and be patient.'

In the event, it was three months before the phone was back in use. One of the hardest things to accept is being cut off from the outside world for long periods at a time. The inability to use the telephone brings this home to you very graphically. There was a time when you could always make a call from the Commodore Hotel, where all the journalists used to stay – they had telexes and international lines; but the Commodore is no more, and there are very few journalists in Beirut now. They come perhaps for a day now and then to cover something special and then get out again as fast as they can.

Refuse is a big problem. It is only collected from time to time and on top of the problems presented by the shelling, the dustmen are frequently on strike for better pay and conditions. So rubbish piles up in the streets and the rats sit on top of it and look at you. I'm told that the cat population has risen in line with that of the rats, but I still think it's a wonder we haven't got cholera here. The piles of rubbish get set alight every so often to minimise the risk, but the sea is full of junk.

I have talked about our problems with gas and electricity. The generator supplied to me by Brent Sadler is a boon for which I cannot adequately express thanks, but whoever designed the pull-string starter was not a woman, let alone a woman like me with a pulled tendon in her shoulder – another riding injury – and its function depends on the supply of benzine, which at the moment, thank God, is sufficient. The thought of sitting alone in the evenings with no distraction and no light except from that damned candle again frightens me.

Day-to-day life is very tense; you cannot trust anyone you meet by chance. A woman came up to me recently, and was charming, very charming, said she knew of my plight, and offered to help in any way she could; but I was so convinced that she belonged to the Syrian Security Police that I snubbed her. Any sudden or unexpected noise makes you jump, even someone dropping their keys on the dark landing outside the flat in the evening – because there is never any electric light there. The only time I feel at home is when I am at the riding club, when I'm with the horses. They, fortunately, have grown so used to the noise of shelling that it no longer frightens them, and Tara is all right as long as she is with me; but it drives Sasha frantic with fear.

It was most unfortunate that during the summer of 1989, immediately following Jackie's kidnapping, I was so alone. Not only all the Europeans, but most of my Lebanese friends left in the face of the fighting, and there was no one about at all. West Beirut was like a ghost town, and you could drive from my flat to Hamra in five minutes – normally, the dense traffic means you need half an hour. In the past couple of weeks, at the time of writing this, everyone has come back, but they may go again. The assassination in West Beirut of President Moawad after only seventeen days in office at the end of November threw everything into confusion again, and heaven knows what will come out of the new president's confrontation with General Aoun.

During the summer, I was virtually the only resident of our block of flats. Walking around the streets, I could not divest myself of the impression that I was being followed – even stalked, and when I got home, there was only Tara to talk to. Yet I had to get my feelings off my chest somehow. I was doubly alone, because no one who has not had the same experience really knows what it is like to be a hostage wife, and I was the only one left in Beirut. If only I had had another woman to talk to – but even Amine's wife, Kay, had left temporarily with the children for safety; and with Amine I have to maintain a stiff upper lip. It is very hard. Then again, there are practical reasons why you cannot communicate – the telephones are out, or it simply is not safe to cross town.

Little things can really bring you down to the depths. You do not sleep well because of the continual shelling, and the five flights of stairs become an unassailable obstacle. You set off shopping, and once you have reached the ground floor, you discover that, because you are tired, you have left your list upstairs. And you just can't face fetching it. Or you had forgotten to switch the car lights off last night, and now the battery's flat: what to do? Nuisances become tortures, and perhaps it all comes back to the shelling. You cannot imagine the horror of lying on a stone floor by yourself under an eiderdown with only a little dog for company, and a cat tearing round the flat like a maniac in fear, unless you have been through it yourself. You cannot even go out on to the landings, or try to reach a neighbour's flat, for fear of flying glass from the corridor windows. But in the morning you pick yourself up, and find that you are still alive, that the shells hit next door. You ask yourself if you can get through one more day – then you discover that there is nothing to eat in the flat, either for the animals or you. You have to pull yourself together and do something about it.

I have found it immeasurably worse than the Blitz, with nothing to save me but Allah and my precious blue bead. If I did not have it, I would go nowhere; I would be too afraid. I have tried to overcome my superstition, but it is too deeply ingrained. I'll never do anything on a Friday the 13th, nor do I ever wear green – I wouldn't even have a green car.

But I won't leave. I know that if Jackie is released, the Syrians will simply come and knock on my door at whatever time of day or night it is, and say something like, 'They're letting him go in Damascus tomorrow morning – get ready to go there now.' And if I am not there at the moment of his release, he will feel terribly let down. I don't know how else he'll feel – he probably won't have any feelings at all; I expect they will have been crushed out of him. But that is why I want to be there, to start helping him immediately to get back to normality. He has always been quite cussed. Because he never learned French, for example, he would never come to dinners or receptions at the French Embassy with me in the old days. But maybe his strength for survival will lie in that very cussedness.

If the worst has happened, and he is dead – well, I have had time to think about that now, and my mind has become clearer since the shelling has eased off for the time being. What I do depends quite simply on money. If I manage to make some from this book, I would like to travel, maybe for six months, just to get away from the whole thing, and everybody; to get away from all the misery, and all the associations I have with this tragedy. I'd like to just *go*, and sort myself out. But it is very difficult to make decisions, and I am still not sure. I'm still in limbo. Even if the news is the worst, I would rather have it than no news at all. Then I could start to put back the pieces. I could stand hearing the worst now. I've had time to adjust, and already I've withstood one false rumour of his death. If that news came again, and was true this time, my grief would not be any less, but I could take it better.

I'm not at all keen on the idea of living in England, but France has a great appeal for me. I'd like to take a cruise before I made any decision – and meet some new people. I love sailing, and it would be nice to be with people who don't know me, who wouldn't talk to me about all this business. The only way I can get through life now is by not dwelling on my problems. If I think about how Jackie is suffering, and what he is going through all the time, it will finish me.

I have an image of him: his routine was to cook his evening meal and have it on a small table in front of the television at about eight each evening. He had his own chair, an armchair with very wide arms, and as soon as he was settled, Sasha would perch on one of the arms next to him, and put her paw out as every forkful was raised. He shared every dinner with Sasha.

9

BOMBINGS AND MASSACRES

In 1981 the Pickwick Bar was blown up by a bomb planted under one of the tables in a plastic carrier-bag. No one was killed, or even badly injured. Jackie wasn't even there – he was on his way, and heard the explosion as he turned the corner into the street where it was. The financial loss represented by the damage to the pub simply had to be written off – there isn't much insurance in Beirut these days; but in any case there was no way of procuring the materials needed for repair, so the Pickwick Bar had to close. Jackie became a bored gentleman of leisure again, doing little apart from tinkering with his balcony-garden. He never really recovered, and I was shocked by the speed with which the experience aged him. I think it was partly because the Pickwick Bar had been a social pivot for him. He maintained a social life with his friends which centred on the Captain's Cabin, and there all the talk was of cricket and football – he followed Northampton and Liverpool – but in time more and more people left, and he was left isolated.

We had no respite then, as not many months were to pass before the Israeli invasion of Lebanon began. Soon they were established in the south of the country, and not long after began their northward advance, with the aim of killing or taking prisoner all Palestinians remaining in Lebanon. The

Palestinians, however, were brave fighters and the battles were fierce. I remember walking my dog one day to find a couple of Palestinians planting anti-tank guns. They were in the way of my habitual walk and I pointed this out to the men, who assured me that the mines were intended for tanks, and would not be triggered by the weight of a human. To prove their point, one of them jumped on one – to no effect, thank heavens.

As the Israelis continued to advance towards Beirut, our Lebanese friends began to pack and leave. It was not long before the bombardment of West Beirut began, I think with the aim of forcing the Lebanese leaders to put pressure on the Palestinians to leave. It was a horrific experience. I vividly remember one occasion during which I spent fourteen hours hiding under a counter in the laundry of our block as the Israeli jets screamed overhead, releasing bombs and rockets. Jackie spent the entire time in the flat, playing Patience. He said that if he was going to be killed, at least he would prefer to die in comfort. I was not so brave, or so stupid. I don't know which.

We eventually had to leave our flat because, owing to the continual shelling, all the windows had been broken and most of the furniture was either damaged or covered with rubble and glass. We went to stay with some flying friends of Jackie's who lived in Hamra Street – Hector was a pilot with MEA, and Elaine was a stewardess. Up to that time, they had been spared most of the shelling, but as soon as we moved, Israeli intelligence discovered that there was a pocket of Palestinian guerrillas holed up in the basement of the block, so they decided to try to flush them out; and the bombs started falling on us again. Elaine and I huddled in a corner with cushions over our heads as some pathetic kind of protection, while Hector and Jackie sat on the balcony drinking beer and watching the pyrotechnics, making such comments as 'That was close!' – close in this case referring to a shell that all but hit Jackie's car, parked outside, and covered mine with rubble. However, after two days of this, Hector and Elaine had had enough, and moved to a small hotel in a quieter district. Jackie and I returned to Raouche.

Everybody was in hiding during the invasion. You were always thinking that your flat or your car was about to be destroyed – indeed, that you would be killed. Survival was a day-to-day, hand-to-mouth business. I clutched my blue bead and prayed to God, to Allah, that the next shell would not be for me – that it would hit my neighbour instead. That was the way one felt in those days – you lived for yourself alone, and you wanted to get out of it alive at all costs. It was a completely different atmosphere from that of the London Blitz, and one's own feelings were different too. Then, everyone helped each other; you shared your ration with the next man or woman, down to your last ounce of butter or your last biscuit. In the Israeli invasion, it was every man for himself. If you had a couple of packets of cigarettes you hid them, and smoked them on your own.

We had to try to patch things up during a lull in the fighting. Jackie went off to look for new glass, and he managed to get the cars going again. I tidied up the flat as best I could – luckily, nothing too precious had been lost, apart from, heartbreakingly, my riding trophies and my photograph albums, since we never had good or new furniture on account of the animals.

It was, of course, very difficult to get down to the riding club at all. I would wait until the shelling stopped – generally around six in the morning – and then make a quick dash out there, keeping my fingers crossed that the enemy was tired and would be having a break for coffee and cigarettes. Each time I arrived, I found things worse and worse – horses would be lying dead in their boxes or, even more sadly, lying with broken legs or backs with half their stables collapsed on top of them. At this time I was greatly helped by Adnan Alamuddine, whose own horse, Sultan, was one of the first to be killed. We took it in turns to run the gauntlet of the Israeli shelling in the mornings. Once on my way home I had to abandon my car and rush into a nearby shop for shelter. That time I was lucky, and my little car escaped damage.

Not surprisingly, there were very few riders at the club. In general, supplies of everything were running low in Beirut – we were effectively under siege. Meanwhile, the Israeli Defence Force was advancing steadily up the country, though they were held up for a while around Damour. Then they came on towards Beirut, and the bombardment was intensified beyond imagination. We had five or six Palestinian fighters in our basement. I used to go down and say, 'Is it safe to take Tara out, do you suppose?' And they would talk to their fellow fighters through their walkie-talkies and say, 'Yes, we think so, for the moment it seems quiet. But don't be too long.' They knew they were beaten, and they were frightened, but they were still brave.

There was a Palestinian arms dump very near the club, and Israeli intelligence got to know about it. They deployed a battery in our direction, and that nearly spelt the end. In the firing over the next two weeks, the club was virtually destroyed. Twenty-two horses were killed, including my own, Gazelle, the last to die. When it was safe to go to the club, Adnan and I did so. The sight that met our eyes was horrible. Many horses were still alive, trapped in their stables, their backs broken, in agony. There was no means of putting them down; we had to watch them die. It might take two days. The clubhouse was half-destroyed. The Israelis achieved their objective too, and blew up the arms dump, but at what cost.

Seven horses survived. Somehow I had to get the club operating again – I had no idea how, but I was determined to do it, and I had the support of Adnan and my old groom, Abu Ali, as well as many other members. Amine Daouk, always my protector and friend, was able to arrange with the owner, Kamal Farajellah, by now in London, to take over the running of the club, and with his help new stables were built, and the rings restored. The clubhouse also rose from its ashes. Meanwhile, I canvassed the old members to see whether they would be prepared to come back. By now, the fighting had died down; a truce had been negotiated, and the PLO had managed to get what they wanted: an honourable withdrawal from Lebanon.

They left with their flags flying, firing their rifles in the air in triumph. For a moment there was a lull.

Eighty per cent of our old riders came back, and several new ones joined us. Soraya, Amine's youngest daughter, now had her own horse, Strand, a magnificent chestnut stallion who had won seven first-class races at the track before it was bombed out. He was then abandoned and left without food, tied to a tree in a small forest on the outskirts of town – a common fate for horses during the war, as there was barely enough food for the people, let alone animals. Soraya had nursed him back to health with loving care, and even given him a scarf to wear in the winter. They had two very happy years together before Strand died, of old age.

An English friend of mine, Susan Barajny, married to a restaurateur called Habil, joined me now and helped me with the training. Meanwhile, I set out to find replacement horses. It was not so easy this time. Very many had been killed – not least in the massacre of the Palestinian refugee camps.

This tragedy occurred as we were just beginning to put the club back on its feet, and it happened on our doorstep, as it were, since the Sabra camp was only two hundred yards from the Arabian Club. The Israelis swore they had nothing to do with the massacres, but they simply turned a blind eye when the Christian Phalangists came down to the camps in September 1982, immediately following the death of Bashir Gemayel. They thought, said the Israelis, that the Phalangists had just come to clear all the remaining Palestinian fighters out of the camps. What followed was wholesale slaughter. They killed everyone, and everything, they could – men, women, children, even animals. Two days later, Abu Ali came up to me at the club in a great state of excitement.

'Come, come! I'll show you what's happened!'

'No,' I said. 'I don't want to see it.'

'Yes, yes – you must come. You must see it!'

Reluctantly, I agreed. There was blood everywhere. Animals, horses, dogs, people. Heads cut off, arms severed. . . . That was

Jack in RAF uniform during World War II.

The wreckage of Jack's plane after it had been shot down in 1941. He took the picture himself, even though he was suffering from terrible injuries.

Jack and Sunnie shortly after their marriage in 1943.

Sunnie greeting Jack on his return from a flight with Middle East
Airlines.

Above: Beirut racecourse in the 1950s (Sunnie had just had her first win on Moussultan).

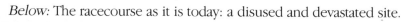

Below: The racecourse as it is today: a disused and devastated site.

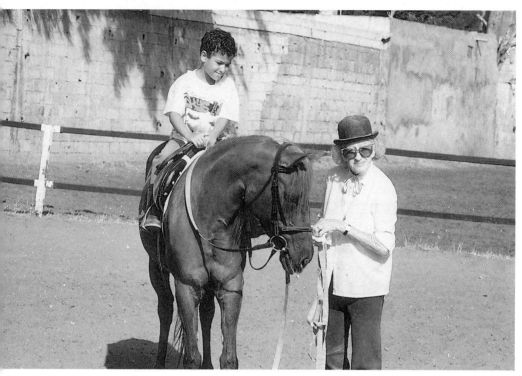

Sunnie giving a lesson at the riding club.

Sunnie with Tara. Behind them are the only riding trophies not to have been destroyed by shelling.

Beirut street scenes.
Above: The familiar sight of the kerosene cart.
Below: Sunnie with a child victim of a shelling.

Jack in the flat, shortly before his abduction.

Sunnie alone in the flat, surrounded by belongings packed up in boxes.

Sunnie as she is today, holding Tara.

as much as I could take. I didn't even go right in – they tell me it was far worse inside. In the hospital, they had even killed patients on the operating tables. The bodies were everywhere – you could hardly walk without stepping on them. Tragically, Abu Ali lost his own son in the scattered fighting that followed this time. He was killed by a stray bullet just outside their house.

Jackie never wanted to know about the massacres.

Shortly after they had occurred, on 23 October 1982, we were riding at the club when we heard a terrific explosion. Somebody had a radio with them and fiddled with it to get a news flash – we were horrified but none of us knew what on earth the bomb's target could have been. It was truly massive. Sure enough, it was soon reported that the US Marine Base by the airport had been blown up. We felt sick; but as we were leading our horses back to the stables there was another explosion – this time the French base near the City Sportive had been attacked. We later learned that 241 marines had been killed by a Hezbollah suicide truck containing 2,000 pounds of explosives. At the French base, 58 paratroopers had been slaughtered.

Still we didn't think of leaving. I think the main objection, though it seems hard to credit it, was that it was such an effort to move. We pondered over it long – how could we move? Who would pack everything up? Where would we find a removal company? There was nothing of the sort in operation. Even if we packed ourselves, how would we possibly take our belongings anywhere? And if we could, where would we go?

Looking for horses to replace those we had lost was a tough job. It was not at all easy then to get up into the Bekaa Valley, where the breeding grounds are and where the best horses are reared. The Syrians controlled the area and it was difficult to get the necessary travel documents. In the end I said, to hell with the Bekaa. I went and looked up Henri Pharon, my old friend from my horseracing days, to ask him if he had any ideas. He told me he had sold some of his horses to a dealer who had them tied up in a small forest not far from the Bourj-el-Barajneh camp. In the company of another friend who is a captain in the Lebanese army I drove down there and struck a deal, paying LL25,000 for two stallions and three mares. Nowadays, that money would not buy you one leg of a horse. They were all thoroughbreds, but in very poor condition after their time in the forest. Nevertheless, you could see that they were beauties – in the outline of their heads and their liquid eyes. Within two months they were as right as rain, and the Arabian Club was properly back in business again.

I hated the Israelis and I hated the period of their occupation, but finally they withdrew to their security zone in the south and we got used to new controllers – the Syrians. For a while, things were peaceful, but peace always seems illusory in Lebanon these days, and it was not long before the tension between Christians and Muslims, and the different Muslim factions, once more began to flare up. The Amal and the Hezbollah started little wars among themselves again, and it was not long before we were to feel the effect of them. Parents withdrew their children from the club, and then adult riders began to stay away.

We had one incident towards the end of 1983, which fortunately did not turn out to be too serious. Four Amal militia men came into the club and announced that they were going to set up a machine-gun in the middle of the jumping ring. I did not say anything, thinking that I had far better keep quiet. I left the club, went straight back home, and rang Amine to tell him what happened.

'We can't have that,' he said. 'If we let them in once, we'll never get them out again. Then more will join them and that'll be the end of the club – and we can't afford that, we've got too many debts to pay off. Leave it to me; I'll make a few phone calls.'

The Amal were there for two days, and then they moved out as abruptly as they had come. They never fired their gun in the daytime when we were there, but only at night.

Nevertheless, we had our share of shelling. At that stage the horses were still unused to it, and the more highly bred among them would become jumpy and go off their feed. It was sad to see them standing well back in their boxes instead of putting their heads out over the doors and looking round.

In general, though, after the Palestinian fighters left, everybody breathed a great sigh of relief. We all started to go out again, and we were shopping and walking around almost normally. Then the Syrians arrived, and I remember that everyone was in two minds about whether this was a good thing or not, though of course there was nothing anyone could do about it one way or the other. The day they came into West Beirut, I was walking my dog along the promenade near our flat. I suddenly heard a great rumbling behind me, and turned to see a whole contingent of tanks coming down the street, with armed soldiers walking alongside. I stopped to chat with a man serving at a coffee van – little mobile stalls which are everywhere in Beirut. He told me that these were the Syrians. The soldiers were all young and extremely nervous, pointing their guns up at the buildings in evident fear of an unexpected terrorist attack. I thought I'd better leave them to it, and made my way home.

For a while, we had a breather after they had arrived. I even stopped carrying the little automatic I'd had right through the time of the Israeli invasion. In any case, I argued, if I ever was picked up and found to have a gun on me, I'd be in really deep trouble.

Living conditions improved. We still had electricity then, though water was already rather scarce. However, then as now, you had to be careful who you talked to about what. The only safe topic of conversation was the Israelis, whom everyone disliked, and you could also curse the militias with caution; but you never said anything against the Syrians, because they had agents everywhere. It's depressing constantly to have to watch your step in conversation – nowadays you dare not express an opinion to total or even relative strangers at all, about anything. For myself, I blame General Aoun for the problems that exist today. I would never live on the East Side. During the Israeli invasion, the West had ninety per cent of the shelling; now the East is getting the worst of it from the Syrians. Most of my friends are on the East Side, and it has been so difficult and dangerous to cross over until very recently that I have not seen some of them for many years. Jackie and I stayed on the West Side because that is where our home is, and where the riding club is. I could not suddenly abandon the West for the East.

There were moves to get the Europeans to leave, but there was no advice. All we had, perhaps three times a week when the British were trying to get their nationals out, was a series of telephone calls from our embassy. The calls were all the same, first from John Grey and then from his successor as ambassador, Alan Ramsay: 'Are you still adamant about not leaving?'

Jackie would reply, 'Yes, we are staying.'

Grey's line then was, 'Don't you think you're being a little foolish? It's very risky for you to stay on, particularly as you are in West Beirut, and the embassy, and all the protection we can offer you, are on the East Side. If anything happens to you there won't be a great deal we can do.'

But we never changed our minds.

The options for us at that stage were not very promising. We could not have moved to another part of Lebanon. To the south, there are the Amal and the Israelis; to the north, the Progressive Socialist Party of the Druze, and the Syrians. We discussed East Beirut, but neither of us really wanted to go there.

At the time of the Sabra massacre the First Secretary got in touch with us and said that he was arranging a convoy of cars to leave all together for Damascus. Everyone had to bring their own petrol and their own cars. Anyone who broke down would be left where they were. Insanely, they gave us only two hours to decide – and it seemed impossible, especially with the animals to consider. We decided against it. I had sold my own small BMW at that time, and Jackie's car was not in the best condition. In the end, I think eight or ten cars went, with everything they could fit in packed in the back. Most of the refugees were British. Now, I sometimes wish that we had gone to Damascus and tried to stay there. But if we had, we would have wanted to come back as soon as the situation appeared hopeful, and if we abandoned the flat even for the shortest time, it would be taken over by squatters, for even now Beirut is still full of dispossessed refugees from the south.

The situation began to get worse. Most of the night you could hear machine-gun fire from the fighting between the Hezbollah and Amal factions. It still was not close to Beirut, but in the suburbs to the south near the airport. However, it was spreading to the refugee camps and I was careful about going out – again. When I thought there was a lull in the fighting, however, I would make a beeline for the club. Luckily, although the camps of Sabra and Chatila, with their wretched surviving inhabitants, were once again targets, the club was not hit at that time.

That did not stop the club's fortunes from taking yet another battering. As the fighting spread, members decided that they had had enough, and withdrew, taking their horses with them, to the East Side. Eventually we lost ten riders and horses, and we once again faced financial difficulties, not least because the grooms could not afford to live on the wages we paid them. Inflation was soaring, everything had gone up by over 700 per cent. All the food they could normally buy cheaply, like bread, rice, fruit and vegetables, came from the south or the mountains, and nothing was arriving, as the roads were blocked. Petrol, too, was in desperately short supply – and a black market started up. Entrepreneurs would stand at the roadside with cans and a placard telling you how much they wanted for 'juice'. If you were absolutely desperate, you paid and you bought it, but you were taking a big chance, because most of the traders had added water to the petrol to maximise their profits. If you were unlucky, you didn't get very far after you had filled up, and it was very risky if you were fleeing from the fighting and your car stopped in a dangerous district, such as Ouzai or Galberi.

Once my car stopped in the middle of an attack, and I knew it was because of the petrol. I got out and abandoned it, thinking

rather the car than me. I went into a nearby house and asked
the occupants if I could shelter with them until the worst of
the fighting had died down, and of course they invited me
in immediately. The Arabs are the most hospitable people on
earth. Once things had calmed down a bit outside, I went out
again, and I was amazed to find that my car had not been
touched. One of the local boys came and blew through the
carburettor and cleared it, so I was able to get home. But
such incidents wear the nerves; I was becoming increasingly
tired and querulous.

Amine told me that we could afford to run the club as a
going concern for another six months; if after that things had
not calmed down, we would have to cut our losses and abandon
the venture. We awaited the outcome of events. There followed
an astonishing number of painstakingly negotiated cease-fires,
some of which lasted only two hours. No one among the
ordinary Lebanese, from breadsellers to professors, had any faith
in them at all. The militias love fighting – after so many years it
has become their job. If there were no fighting and peace came,
what would they do? Who would pay them fighting money?
No one. They would be out of a job, and they would end up
standing around on street corners, all their importance gone.
So, they wanted to keep the fighting going. We all knew this,
so no one was remotely surprised when after a few hours, or
days, we were all back where we started.

But the seventh cease-fire held. An instinct born of bitter
experience had taught me when it was safe to go out, and when
not. I have got used to driving through firing in the course of
so many variations on the theme of war, and I always bear in
mind that when they have a heavy battle at night, they are tired
in the early morning, as a rule. After all, they have been busy all
night, with no time for sleep or a cup of coffee. So they would
nearly always have a break around dawn. Then you generally
got three or four hours of relative calm. I would dash out and
do what I had to do, then get back in again. The shops opened
before seven in Beirut, so you could manage your shopping

before the resumption of hostilities, or go to the club to check the horses.

I am not outstandingly brave. Jackie always said I was stupid to keep on going to the club all the time; but as I have said before, my heart is with animals, and the pull of animals – in this case, the horses – which I might be able to save, to feed, overcame my fear of the shelling. So I kept on going. Of course I was frightened – you would be a fool if you weren't frightened when you heard the shells coming. Often I would drive home as if I were back in an ambulance during the Battle of Britain, weaving from side to side along the road so as not to provide a direct target. I've had a few near misses, but I'm still here – touch wood!

On one occasion not so very long ago, during fighting between the militias, I arrived at the club to find that a shell had smashed a stable. The roof had collapsed on the horse inside, breaking its back. The only other person there at the time was one of the grooms called Mahmoud, and as he and I together were not strong enough to lift the heavy eternite slabs off the horse, he said he would go to fetch help. I waited about half an hour and then, as he still had not come back, I went after him. I found him not far away, lying at the side of the road, his leg shattered by a sniper's bullet. I then had to find somebody to help me get him into my car, and took him to hospital. This is the kind of incident that one has to take in one's stride. Life is very cheap in Beirut, and the butchery and savagery are hard to come to terms with. I think of the driver of the suicide lorry that blew up the American marines. The driver had to come quite a long way to get to their base. What can his thoughts have been on the journey?

The sad thing is that the children here are growing up in this atmosphere of violence. You see even little ones, three-year-olds, girls and boys, playing soldiers. You never see them playing with dolls, or kicking a ball around. No, they have bits of wood which they use as toy machine-guns, and they shoot you with them as you pass them in the street. They are simply imitating what they see every day.

Increasingly I find myself an odd woman out in Beirut. People often look at me strangely. Obviously I feel very different now from how I used to, after fifteen years of living in the middle of a war. The carefree days of cocktail parties and dinners out and ambassadors' receptions are over and gone. I don't want to go anywhere, these days. All I want to do after I get home safely is to sit down with my glass of beer at home. If you do meet up with your friends, you do so at lunchtime, never in the evenings. But I have got strangely used to this life, and although I am English, I have a deep fellow feeling for the Lebanese people. I have always loved Lebanon. Now, most of my friends are Lebanese. They are very loyal. I have found that out.

Our flat is very simply furnished. What we have has literally been through the wars, and as Sasha uses everything as a scratching post, Jackie has always maintained that there is no point in replacing anything. We enjoy our glass of beer, we both smoke, and Jackie likes his whisky, and exotic things like English pork sausages and tinned steak and kidney pies, which he buys at great expense from Smith's; but otherwise we live simply.

Occasionally our fairly tight economy has come in for a shock. For example, the last quarterly telephone bill was for LL100,000. I almost fainted when I opened the envelope, as our usual bill is around the five thousand mark. When I showed it to Jackie, he said, 'What the hell have you been doing? Who have you been phoning?'

'I haven't phoned anyone – just local calls.'

We looked at the bill more closely, and there were listed calls to Cairo, England, America, Germany – you name the place, and it was on our bill. What had happened was that one of the militias had tapped into our line. It is something that happens in Beirut; people do it with the electricity supply too.

I talked to Amine about it – I always go to Amine when there is anything wrong. He said, 'I know the head of the telephone company – I'll have a word.' To begin with, their response was that they were terribly sorry, but *someone* had to pay for the calls, and it wasn't going to be them. We told them again that we hadn't made even one of the long-distance calls, and with Amine exerting a little influence in the background, they halved the bill; but it was still a lot of money.

When there were regular flights in and out of Lebanon, Jackie would go to Cyprus for two months every year, and I went to England. Thinking about it, I realise that even if we wanted to, we could not live in England now, because we simply could not afford it. In any case, we have nothing in England; we would be fish out of water. Jackie did look around at prices in Cyprus when he was last there. He went into some detail, looking at the prices of food and drink as well. When he came back, he said, 'We can't afford to live in Cyprus either!' That was all right by me. I didn't want to go to live in Cyprus. If I have to live in the heat, it is just as hot in Cyprus as in Beirut. And what would I do in Cyprus? There is no riding to speak of, and I cannot play tennis any more. I don't care for swimming, so I expect I would end up going for endless walks, and doing a bit of shopping. So – I am trapped in Beirut. I suppose I will end my days here; but I don't know what will happen any more. If and when Jackie comes home I might feel differently. I am tired, and all I can do is wait and see.

There are very few foreigners in Beirut now. Only three or four European wives of Lebanese are left, but I do not lack for company. I speak fluent French, and enough Arabic to get by – though I could not hold a very involved conversation in it. Looking back, I have few regrets. We had a perfectly happy life in Lebanon, and I have been able to devote myself to horses. As for the factions, I cannot say that I fear one more than another. If anything – *if* – I would say that I feel more cautious about the Syrians than about any one militia group. I have not personally had any really unpleasant times with the militias.

Before General Aoun's War of Liberation, we were still not very comfortable; day-to-day living was difficult. We only had electricity for six hours a day – though if we had that much now we would think it marvellous. A daily rota was published in the newspaper, covering all the districts of West Beirut. You would read: *Raouche: Monday, 6 am–12 noon*, for example. And that way, you would be able to plan your day around the supply. I might plan to make a dent in the great pile of laundry – depending on the availability of water. Or we might decide to do the shopping – especially the heavy stuff, like the petfood tins – so that we could get it upstairs in the lift. If the electricity supply was on early, Jackie would have to get up well before his usual time, and he would grumble terribly.

If there was enough water available to do washing, he would have to collect it and fill the washing machine – they take an enormous amount, about five twenty-litre cans – and it takes time to fill them. To maximise the time, Jackie might do the washing while I shopped. If I was lucky, I'd get some ironing in too.

As the electricity supply got worse, so did our water situation. With six hours' electricity, we were usually able to get the cans up to the flat in the lift, and in those days there was a standpipe in the basement. But at about the same time that the electricity was reduced, the water was cut off. Trying to keep clean became a nightmare, because you could not afford to use much of your precious supply for washing. We would argue:

'Damn it,' Jackie would say, 'I haven't had a bath for four days.'

'Well really, dear, you don't need a bath as much as I do,' I'd reply. 'You're sitting here all day. I'm out in the dirt and dust at the riding school. I need a bath more.'

Then there would be a short silence before he said: 'All right – I'll have the bath first, then you can get in.'

'No, no,' I'd reply. 'I don't think so. I don't think that's a good idea at all.'

'All right! You have the damned bath! I'll go without! I'll smell! I'll put scent on instead!'

If getting stuck in the lift, my greatest fear, happened, even though I have always been swiftly rescued, so far, my clothes would be filthy from clambering out – and there would be no means of washing them. Also, while Tara and I could make our escape, we very often had to leave all the shopping in the lift until the electricity came on again the following day. Much of the food would have spoiled in the heat by then.

There was never any hope of bathing Tara – she got dirtier and dirtier. In the end, I became so desperate that I took her round to Amine's place, and said to Kay, 'Can I please bath Tara here? I just can't stand the smell of her any more.' They have a generator, something which we could not afford, and at the time did not have. A big generator costs thousands of dollars, and even a small one just to run the lighting costs five hundred. We used to sit at night with candles. No television, no video, and not enough light to read by. Just endless games of 'Boggle', which Jackie always won. Our refrigerator worked for the six hours when the electricity was on, and you could have a beer that was not tepid then. But when electricity was cut to one hour, even that became an impossibility. Sometimes the electricity supply was rostered to our district at a ridiculous time of day, like midnight to 6 am. A whole host of petty difficulties wore us down.

After General Aoun, in his struggle against the Syrians, put the Christians of the East Side on to a war footing with the Muslim population of the West, many of our supplies, which came through the East Side port, were cut off. Fruit and vegetables, usually plentiful, were in short supply; bread was virtually unobtainable, and the beer depot closed because no fresh crates had been delivered. Stocks on supermarket shelves thinned out dramatically. Soon we were down to an hour's electricity a day and with twenty apartments in our building, the competition for the lift when it was working was intense. You might stand at the bottom with your water cans and wait five, ten, fifteen minutes for it to arrive. It was frustrating and enervating. Finally one day at the club Amine came up to me and said, 'Sunnie, you're looking very depressed. What's the matter?'

'You'd be looking depressed,' I replied, 'if you'd been through what I went through yesterday, trying to get enough water to cook a cauliflower, let alone wash myself.'

'Well, why on earth don't you come round to my place with your cans – there's a well; you can fill your cans up and drive them back in your car.'

'That's a wonderful idea. Thank you.'

We loaded all our cans that afternoon, drove round to Amine's, filled them up, and then tore back to the flat to catch the lift. After that, it became a habit, for Amine lived much closer than the other water at least notionally available, at the club. Sometimes we caught the lift; other times, we were less lucky. Then it was terrible.

One day, the Zouk power station was shelled. As there was consequently no more supply from there, everyone was drawing on the one remaining station. The result was that all power was cut completely for three days. Mercifully we still had a few bottles of butane gas, but because it got dark by 6.30 pm, Jackie had to change his routine and have his main meal at lunchtime, for at night there was not enough light to cook by. Laundry became increasingly difficult, even when power was restored. We worked through all our clothes, and our four sets of sheets and pillowcases. By the time everything had been used, and there was still no chance of getting anything clean, I swallowed my pride again and threw myself on Amine's mercy. Being the friends they are, the Daouks let me spend a whole day with them, using their washing machine.

The one hour of electricity we were getting by now was scheduled for equally dotty times; 1 to 2 am was quite a favourite. But I was damned if I was getting up in the middle of the night to do ironing.

Jackie would go shopping three hours before the current

was scheduled to come on, to dovetail his arrival back with the lift working; but half the time this plan misfired. I was better suited to the hardships than he was, because I have always taken exercise, and eaten and drunk little; even so I was frequently exhausted. It was hell for him. Those stairs became a torment, even for the younger tenants. We all found we could cope for a few days, but after a few weeks, a few months, you found yourself in a state of near-collapse. 1989 was the worst year to date. General Aoun insists that he is the true leader of the country, refuses to recognise the government, says it is a Syrian puppet, and the fight continues, each side of the city shelling the other mercilessly. How long can it go on?

At the time we were going through such misery, I had a telephone call from the British Ambassador on the East Side. He told me that over there they were getting twelve hours' electricity a day – most of the power is supplied from the East Side – but that Aoun had no intention of easing up on hostilities. Once again he suggested that we leave; once again we refused to budge. However, it looked as though we had a very unpleasant time ahead of us. Jackie remained optimistic at first, and said that things could never be as bad again as they were in the Israeli raids, but petrol supplies dried up once more, and it became increasingly difficult to get to the club. I managed to scrounge the odd twenty litres through riding friends who had contacts in the garages, but it was not a regular supply.

Then the bombardment of the East by the West began. The first attack must have lasted five days without a let up. All the residents of East Beirut cowered under cover. On the West Side we thought, very unkindly of course, 'Well, now it's your turn. We had it all through the Israeli invasion.' And we congratulated ourselves on having stayed on the West Side. We listened to the radio news from East Beirut. It was often read – still is – by a very dramatic-sounding girl called Magda Tacher. To hear her speak, you would have thought the sun shone out of General Aoun's *derrière*. It was hilarious – the only laugh of the day we had. If she came on I'd shout across to Jackie to come and listen. It was a treat. She would begin by saying something like, 'The Syrian army of occupation has been shelling the residents of East Beirut for the past eight hours.' We knew that they had been shelled, and we were sorry for them, but the sound of this heavily dramatic voice was too much. You would have thought no one had ever been shelled in Beirut before. She announced that Aoun would carry on: Beirut, in its history, had already been destroyed and rebuilt fifteen times. If need be, it would be again. Both Jackie and I answered more or less in unison, 'Yes, but what about rebuilding the people who are getting killed?'

In April 1989 the situation in Beirut deteriorated rapidly. The Syrians were continuing to shell the eastern half of the city every day. Aoun had got tired of this, I presume, and thought it was time that he retaliated. We on the West Side duly started getting shelled. I was on the beach one day with Tara, who was enjoying herself as usual, chasing crabs. There were quite a lot of cars parked on the promenade, and people were sitting about, having coffee and chatting. Suddenly out of the calm blue sky we heard the noise of a shell. The people abandoned their coffee and started to run for cover, but there was nowhere, except by the little coffee vans. I yelled at Tara to come to me but she was miles away and I was not going to leave without her. The shell hit while I was still on the beach, but luckily on the far side of the promenade. The building whose side it had hit promptly collapsed. Nobody knew if there were any people inside, and nobody stayed to find out. Everyone made a dash for their cars. In the evening, we heard on the news that the shell had killed two people. It had been unpleasantly close.

A few days later I had an even closer shave when I returned with Tara in the car after a walk on the beach. I had a beige Renault 12, and had just parked it, not far from the flat. We had not gone more than two hundred yards when we heard the unmistakable hissing noise of shells. I picked Tara up and was just about to start running when the first one landed. It landed right on top of the car. My little Renault went up in the air like a feather, gently, turned round three times and then fell to the ground on its back. I was shaking by this time. It was only by the grace of Allah that we had not still been in the car, after all. I got back to the flat, after clambering up the five flights as usual, and walked into the *salon* on tottering legs. It was still relatively early, and Jackie was sitting up in bed having his breakfast.

'We're back,' I said.

'Good.'

'We're back safely,' I said more slowly.

He looked at me. 'Good,' he repeated.

I said, 'For Christ's sake, you lie in your goddam bed – didn't you hear anything? Didn't you hear the shells coming down?'

'Yes, I heard them.'

'Well, one came down on my car!'

'What?'

'Yes, on my car; and Tara and I had just got out.'

'Well,' he said, 'aren't you lucky you're not dead? After all, you were out of the car – you're here, alive and kicking.'

'Yes,' I replied, 'I was out of the car; but how the bloody hell do you think I'm feeling?'

He looked blank. 'Would you like a cup of coffee or something?'

I sighed. 'Never mind, dear. Just go back to your breakfast and your crossword. I'll get myself a stiff brandy.'

Jackie was being his usual offhand self, and I should not have minded. He got up immediately, went round to our garage and asked Mahmoud there to look out another car for me. It was not too hard because so many people who have left the country deposited their cars at various garages for sale if possible. Jackie found me a Honda Accord, drew money from the bank to pay for it, did so, and brought it back the same day. I was very touched. I knew, too, that I partly deserved his offhand treatment. He is not insensitive, but he does think that I'm accident-prone, and I have never broken down in front of him. I'm not a person to cry. These things can happen to me and two hours later I'll be laughing them off with friends.

Whenever we had a quarrel – and we had as many as any other husband and wife – I used to think, I wish to God I was out of here, and having a nice, happy, peaceful life with electric light, and water on tap, somewhere else. But that was just a reaction of the moment. I never seriously contemplated throwing the towel in. One or two people who have left Beirut and then returned briefly to collect belongings have said that they are sorry to be away – they find life dull, especially those who have returned to England. It's almost unbelievable but they seem to miss the excitement; and it is true that somehow the constant danger keeps you going. If there is a lull for two or three weeks, people will start to say things like, 'It's a bit boring now, isn't it? Nothing's going on.'

Perhaps I was wrong earlier. Perhaps there is a camaraderie. Some of my neighbours in Jaroudy Buildings have been there ten or twelve years, and I've never known them except to pass the time of day; and yet when Jackie was kidnapped, they all came round to see if there was anything they could do.

It is fairly quiet in my district at the moment. If you drive south towards Khalde you sometimes get stopped by a Muslim militia checkpoint near the Summerland Hotel, which is a huge luxury place that somehow manages to keep going, and then it is very hot and irritating, waiting as they go through everyone's papers. In general, driving in Beirut is grim, though on a good day I can get to the club in twenty minutes. The worst road hogs are the service taxis. They charge along, but if they see a prospective passenger they will slam on the brakes and reverse back to them – and it's up to you to get out of the way. I give them a wide berth. Formerly, service taxis all had red licence plates so you knew where you were with them, but now anyone who wants to seems to be able to go into the taxi business for himself. It makes life very hazardous.

Nevertheless, I always try to be as nice as I can when I'm

on the roads – I think it's the best policy. Jackie, on the other hand, always got very aggressive, especially if he was stopped at checkpoints, and if they shouted, he would shout back. I smile and occasionally stop for a chat in Arabic. I have always found that helps. If I am coming back late from the club, around half past five, there is always a big traffic jam caused by a Syrian checkpoint. Nowadays I generally pull out and drive to the front of the queue. The Syrians know me, and wave me on. That saves a lot of wear and tear on the nerves, because when you are stuck in your car in a queue you are always afraid of shells, and if shelling actually does start, the panic is grim. Everyone panics and tries to force the queue forward, sounding his horn. But we survive, and I do not think I could go home to the UK, even to stay with my family, although I love them dearly. How they used to envy us, living in Lebanon.

Of course, once the situation here changed, so did family opinion. My brother Glyn especially would write constantly, 'Are you really staying on? . . . Why don't you move. . . . It's getting too dangerous out there . . .'. And, as matters got steadily worse, 'Why don't you leave? . . . What on earth makes you stay in a place like that? . . . If it's money you're worried about, I can help you. . . . Come back to England and leave everything. Although you won't admit it, I know the real reason you won't come is that you won't leave your animals; but it's only six months' quarantine for Tara, that isn't a lifetime!' Then he'd put a PS for Jackie: 'The climate here isn't as bad as you think – we do get some summer, and if you lived in the south I think it would be quite bearable for you.'

Now that Jackie has gone, the family have redoubled their efforts to get me home; but Glyn knows me and he is quite right – I will not leave the horses, and Tara and Sasha are family to Jackie and me. I certainly won't go without Jackie, and if he is still alive and comes back to me, he will still be adamant about not returning to England. I know him well enough to know that. As for me, I think I might vegetate in England. I have a zest for life; I love it. I always think that there's something interesting round the next corner, and I like to go and find it. I'm very healthy, and I've never been ill. The only mishaps I've had have been riding accidents, and they go with the job. Luckily food does not interest me much, and I really only eat salads and fruit. But what really keeps me young is that I work all the time with young people, children and teenagers.

Above all, life here is never boring. There are bad moments, but you have to try to keep them at bay. I get through my day fairly well. By the time I have taken Tara for a walk and done some shopping, the morning is taken care of, and in the afternoons I ride, or, if the shelling is too heavy to get down to the club, I will have a siesta. The danger lies in the long evenings. At least now with my generator I can watch a video.

The worst thing is having no distraction from one's grief. It is difficult to describe how the wife of a hostage feels. For the first two days after Jackie was taken I seemed to be in limbo, doing what Amine told me, and allowing myself to be guided by the one friend among the horde of journalists who besieged me immediately after the kidnapping – Julie Flint of the *Guardian*. All I could think about was – is Jackie alive? How is he? Is he chained to a bed in some small underground room? How will he communicate with his kidnappers, having no Arabic or French? I worried about his loathing of Arabic food, about how he would miss his beer and whisky, about how he would manage without cigarettes, if they decided not to give him any. I was demented with worry, and could neither eat nor sleep.

My one real consolation was Tara. I could allow myself to cry in front of her, and I talked to her as if she were a human being. By great good fortune, Kay Daouk returned from England with the children soon after, and it was a comfort to have another woman to confide in, though my neighbour Fadya kept inviting me down to her apartment too, for a chat and a cold beer – she had a generator, and my own beer was warm all the time. As now, the evenings were the worst, but then they were insupportable, and if it hadn't been for Amine's constant visits and telephone calls I doubt if I would have kept my sanity.

Julie Flint was a saint, too, and had lighting which ran off a car battery installed in my flat – just having proper light in the evenings made a world of difference.

Since that time I have been waiting, and holding on.

Things have not let up much. One recent awful memory I have is of a car-bomb that went off opposite our flats. One of the little coffee vans that sell refreshments had parked on the sea promenade in Raouche, and the car-bomb stood midway between it and the Syrian checkpoint, a couple of hundred yards away. When it blew up I was in the flat. I thought it was shelling, the noise was so loud. I went out on to the balcony and saw what had happened. The coffee van was engulfed in flames. Two or three people ran out of our flats to help. It was ghastly. People had been sitting around at tables by the sea. Three men had been blown right out over the sea and smashed against the Pigeon Rocks. Two children were blasted into the sea. At the checkpoint, two Syrian soldiers had been killed. This is how things continue to be in Beirut.

10

HOLDING ON

I must go back to the days following Jackie's kidnapping. To begin with, as I have said, I never seemed to know what I was doing. I would pick up a dustpan and brush, and a minute later have no idea what I was going to do with them. Nothing seemed to register. Somehow I got through the first night, mainly because of Tara. If she hadn't been there, I don't know what I would have done. I sat up most of the night talking to her, telling her that tomorrow he would be back. He would walk into the flat with one of her favourite bones.

I got up at 5.30 am. At 7.00 the doorbell rang. It was Amine. He stayed with me for an hour, advising me and telling me what to do. Not to go out. Whatever happened, not to open the door. To put the chain lock on. He would be back later.

At noon there was a terrible hammering and thundering and kicking at the door. People outside were shouting and screaming. I was very afraid. I didn't open the door. I went out on to the balcony in the front of the building. Below, I could see a large number of men with cameras, aiming them up at me. Other neighbours were leaning over their balconies to see what was going on. I could see other men walking backwards and forwards, carrying equipment of some kind into our building. I went back into the flat. The noise from

136

beyond the front door now was really appalling. They were shouting, 'We want a photograph!' My nerves had reached such a state that I couldn't stand it any more. I opened the door, leaving the chain on. I shouted at them to go away and come back tomorrow. 'I can't talk today,' I said. It was no good. Then, among them I saw a woman's fair hair.

'Are you English?' I shouted.

She was. I asked her to come in and slipped the chain to allow her to do so. Another reporter jammed his foot in the door so that I couldn't close it. I had closed Tara in the bedroom, but now I asked the woman to let her out. Once she was free, Tara started barking fiercely. The Lebanese reporter took his foot out of the door and retreated. I slammed it shut. Julie Flint, as she introduced herself to me, stayed with me most of the day. Amine joined us as he had promised and between them they worked out a plan of action for me. I would have to face the press sooner or later. It was decided that I should give a statement the next morning at eleven. With their help, I got through that first encounter, but I now find it much easier to sympathise with Royalty when they say they have had enough of being badgered by the press. In their quest for photographs, these people had ransacked my remaining albums, and I was too shaken to stop them.

Amine foraged for beer for me, and managed to come up with a whole case. Julie, who was experienced in hostage negotiation, stayed with me all evening, together with her cameraman, Khaseem, and said that she would find out what she could through her contacts.

The days seemed to melt into one. We drove round to meet one or two minor Syrian officials, who said they would do their best to help, though they had heard nothing about Jackie through their own intelligence network. Then, on the third day, a Syrian soldier arrived at the flat, and with Khaseem as interpreter explained that they had found Jackie's Simca. Usually, the car would be taken with the hostage, but as they had found it, they were returning it to me. I was not to use it, however, and I was to keep it hidden. The soldier handed me the keys.

The following day I decided that I simply had to get some food, and prepared to go shopping. I took the bunch of car keys – I had keys on my ring for both the Honda and the Simca – and went round to the back of the flats to get a basket I needed which I knew was in Jackie's car. As I went to open the boot I saw that a key was broken off in the lock. Suddenly I realised why they hadn't taken the car. Jackie also had keys for the Honda on his car key-ring. The terrorists, whose usual ploy is to shove their victim into the boot of his own car and drive off with it, had mistakenly tried to open the boot with the Honda key. It had broken off. I rang a Syrian army major who had already interviewed me and told him what I had discovered.

'That confirms exactly what we've just heard,' he said. 'We have three witnesses to the kidnapping. They came upon the kidnappers doing exactly what you describe. When they were surprised, the kidnappers panicked and pushed your husband into their own car, then drove off.'

I was relieved, because if they had succeeded in pushing Jackie into the Simca's boot, he would not have survived. He isn't capable of bending at all, and he would have had a heart attack if forced to. He has already suffered one slight stroke.

I got Mahmoud to come round from the garage and open the boot. There was nothing in the car, so Jackie can never have got to the supermarket; but he'd been to the bank and got out the money he'd wanted – he'd cashed a cheque for £100. The empty shopping basket was in the boot. I suddenly saw him in my mind's eye, dressed as he was that day – in blue slacks, check shirt, and beige pullover. I wonder what he's wearing now, after all this time?

The embassy rang with a message of sympathy from the Ambassador, and offers of help – he was even prepared, very kindly, to have me as his guest for as long as I wished. I thanked them, but explained that I had to stay put, in case any news came through.

Amine told me that if we had not had any demands for money within a week, we would not be looking at a straightforward ransom kidnap, but he advised me to broadcast an appeal immediately, stressing that we had no money and lived simply. This I did, to no avail, either way. Julie through her contacts had established that Jackie had not been taken by the Hezbollah; it seemed that he was the prisoner either of Palestinians or of some unidentified maverick group. It was all guesswork, though, and to this day I don't know who is holding him. There has been no direct signal from them.

Julie advised me to make another appeal, this time directly to the Syrians, whom she was convinced were the ones who would be able to help me, if anybody could. I followed Julie's advice, making myself look as bad as possible for the cameras, taking off my make-up and pulling the combs from my hair. But this appeal had no more effect than the first. Slowly, desperation began to sink into me. The hours at home were long, though when you have animals you have to look after them, and that helps pull you together. But I was unaware of myself.

'Don't you have another shirt?' Julie asked me one day.

'Certainly. Why?'

'I think you might feel better if you changed the one you've got on. You've been wearing the same clothes for three days.'

After that, I pulled myself together a little, and began to feel marginally better. About the same time Julie produced the delightful surprise of the car battery-run lighting. That made an enormous difference to my outlook, and I pulled myself together properly, and went out to see people on my own account. I even tried to contact the head of the Amal, Nabih Berri, but he was always either in Damascus or the south. In June, an interview was arranged for me with the head of Syrian Intelligence, after some effort on my part. I had a complete body search before the interview; apparently he changes buildings every two or three days – he has three palatial flats – for fear of assassination.

We were ushered into an office, sat down, and soon afterwards he entered. He was most charming, and we tried to manage without an interpreter, but his French wasn't up to it, and nor was my Arabic. He said that they would do all they could. I had made an appeal on Jackie's birthday – 11 June – which he had seen, and he told me that they were doing, and would do, everything they could.

'I have one small ray of hope for you,' he said. 'We've picked up one of the kidnappers and we're holding him for questioning. There is just a chance that they may contact us to try to exchange Jackie for the man we are holding. But don't expect it to happen quickly. Things like this take time. Don't expect to see Jackie home within days.'

I left feeling a little better, but of course nothing has come of it since.

I go on waiting. What worries me the entire time is, how is Jackie coping now? I feel guilty every time I drink a glass of beer. I remember how he loved his beer, and I feel sure he's not getting any. His temperament worries me too. He is very easy-going up to a certain point, but after that his temper is explosive, like a little brain-storm. I think, what if the kidnappers irritate him in some way – perhaps he'll ask for non-Arab food, and they won't give it to him. He is liable to flare up and start cursing. What their reaction would be to that I just don't know. They may hit him, or tie him up. I don't know, and I am afraid. If he is chained and blindfolded, then I am certain he will have a second stroke, and that could finish him.

What gives me hope is that Jackie is a survivor. It showed when he was a fighter pilot. He can be difficult over little things, but when it really matters, he is tremendous. I think if the kidnappers treat him reasonably well, he'll come through. I miss him every day. We have been married for forty-six years, and perhaps we were inclined to take each other for granted. But Jackie was there when the washing machine refused to work, or when I had a flat tyre, or when Zara was killed. Now I am alone and have to fight the daily battles without a shoulder to cry on.

I have tried to keep to my usual routine, as the weeks have stretched into months, and take Tara out for her regular morning walk – but at first even getting out of the flat was an ordeal. The Lebanese are always very interested in other people's troubles, and I would be stopped perhaps ten times by people asking if there was any fresh news of Jackie. Although it was done with the best of intentions, it only added to my misery. I half-heartedly dust the flat, just keeping the dust level down. Anything more than that is beyond me.

Amine suggested that I start riding again two or three times a week. His idea was that working with the children would distract me from brooding, and he was absolutely right. When you are teaching six- and seven-year-olds to ride you have to concentrate completely, or they are likely to fall off if the horse does something unexpected; then you have a screaming child and a frantic mother on your hands, both wishing horses had never been born. That's not good publicity for a riding club. I was also helped a great deal by Mehdi, the ITN cameraman who works closely with the television reporter Brent Sadler – both were to become good friends. Mehdi would frequently drive me off to dangerous bombed-out areas to get a photograph of me standing in front of a pile of rubble that was once a house, with my knees shaking and my nerves in shreds, because I knew that at any moment the Amal and the Hezbollah would start shooting at each other again, and Mehdi and I might well disappear under some more rubble.

In the meantime, my daughter and my brother were redoubling their efforts to get me to leave Beirut and return to England. I couldn't do it. The international airport was in any case now closed, and England was too far away to get back to Beirut quickly if there were some positive news of Jackie. So I decided to stick it out, although this was not the easiest of decisions to make. Almost every day battles were being fought in different areas, and avoiding lethal car-bomb attacks was purely a question of luck. If I saw an empty car parked on an almost deserted street, I would turn round and go back the way I came. I'm terrified of car-bombs – more so than the shelling. You have no chance whatsoever if a car-bomb goes off as you are passing – they are devastating, indescribable in their effect; the damage and the panic they inflict are nightmarish. I wondered what Jackie would do if I were killed and there was no one to meet him on the day of his release; and I worried about the fate that would befall Tara and Sasha if I were not around to look after them. I kept wishing that I could talk to other hostage wives and mothers, to find out what their reactions were during the first weeks of being alone, but those who had lived here had left, and the others lived too far away.

It took me a month before I was able to face life again with any semblance of control. Now, months have passed, and as far as most people are concerned, the excitement is over. Jackie is no longer news, because there is nothing to report. I find now that I miss this, much as I disliked the attentions of the press when the story 'broke', and I try to keep Jackie's name before the public as much as I can. I was most distressed when in his service to mark 1,000 days of captivity for Terry Waite, the Archbishop of Canterbury also mentioned Brian Keenan and John McCarthy, but not Jackie.

As the Lebanese summer got into its stride and the weather became ever hotter, I grew increasingly exhausted. Because of the dearth of electricity, even food kept in the fridge went bad after thirty hours. The arrival of the generator, so kindly organised for me by Brent, was a godsend; but then supplies of benzine for it ran low. There were evenings when I just sat looking at the candle, too tired and depressed even to talk to Tara. Shelling would start in the small hours, so sleep became impossible. I considered moving to Cyprus, but the animals presented a problem, for they would have to go into quarantine; then I discovered that in any case I had not enough money to rent a flat in Larnaca in high season. This book became more and more of a lifeline. When I first discussed it with Brent, it was to have been the story of my riding experiences in Lebanon.

Some of that has remained, but how different the circumstances which would affect its contents were to become.

As the weather grew steadily hotter, I worried more and more about the conditions in which Jackie was being held. As my own anxiety and tiredness increased, I once again entered a kind of limbo, performing my tasks and duties as if in a trance, and barely able to drag myself around for Tara's two daily walks. There were days when the thought of walking her in the heat of August was enough to reduce me to tears, but she had to go out, so off we would go.

I longed for news, either from Julie Flint, who had by now left Beirut, or Brent. Worst of all were the nights. I have spent more now than I can count lying in the corridor of the flat, away from all the windows, shaking with fear. But even that I could stand if I were not alone. In mid-July, I spent the most miserable birthday of my life, with only Tara and a candle for company. During that summer, as the hostilities between east and west grew fiercer, it became impossible even to ride, and there was no point in going down to the club as no one would be there. So I lost my one diversion from the grimness of life in West Beirut.

But I take comfort from the letters of sympathy that I receive, many from people I have never met, and the fact that other people – even relative strangers – do care about my plight. I keep every letter, and I hope that when Jackie is released I will be able to answer every one and thank my correspondents for their support during these ghastly months. There is one thing I disagree with; people tell me that once Jackie is with me again I will look back on these terrible days as at a bad dream; but I know differently. These months are etched on my heart, and I will not forget them until I die. The continuous shelling, and the lack of water, food and electricity have taken their toll on me over the last few months, and made me realise my age at last. That has only added to my depression. I keep thinking, despite everything, of what I could be doing if I were in England. Having a daily bath – what luxury! Being able to watch television whenever I wanted to. Going to the cinema! I could see my daughter, visit my grandchildren. I could even go to one of England's beautiful pubs and have a glass of beer without the fear of a sudden shell falling on me. But then I come out of my dream world and feel selfish. Jackie has to go without all those things too, and has the additional horror of being a captive. And once more I face the fact that I cannot leave, and that somehow I must find the strength and determination to stick it out until he is released.

One night not so long ago I was awoken by knocking at my front door, and Tara barking furiously. It was 11 pm, and I had gone to bed at 9.30 in order to get some sleep before the shelling started. Brent had already told me that the Syrians would contact me as soon as there was any news of Jackie, day or night, so I went to answer the door, Tara under my arm, torch in hand; but I kept the chain on, and shone my torch on to the face of the man standing outside. I was very scared. He began speaking in Arabic, but I asked him to switch to English.

'You are Mrs Sunnie Mann?'

'Yes.'

'We need to look at your husband's car.'

'At this time of night?'

'We need to look at his car.'

I looked into the darkness behind him. There were other men there. Tara is very small, but she makes a lot of noise. I put her down on the floor and she moved into the opening of the door. The men instinctively stepped back, and I slammed the door and locked it. I was petrified and did not know what to do. There was silence in the darkness. I poured myself a large brandy to calm myself, and sat down.

This was not the first time I had been awakened in the middle of the night. Once before, there had been a telephone call at one am.

'Mrs Mann?'

'Yes.'

The phone went dead. I now feel very frightened of being

alone in the flat, but I don't know what to do about it, as there is no one left in Beirut who can come to stay with me. I suppose I shall have to get used to it. I pray that Jackie will soon be free and home again, so that I can keep my sanity.

Brent arrived in East Beirut, and Mehdi, Tara and I set off to cross over to see him. Our rendez-vous was the Montemar Hotel in Jounieh. At the time, there were several television crews in Jounieh, as news of the murder of the American army officer, Colonel Higgins, had just broken. I myself gave three interviews to different networks, appearing as I always do with Tara, to keep Jackie's name before the public. I also enjoyed, as I always do when I get away from West Beirut, the luxury of a hotel bathroom.

The following morning I had to return to West Beirut, and as usual I was extremely nervous about making the crossing. Until very recently there has always been a serious risk of being hit by sniper fire, and Mehdi has scars in his calf from the time when a bullet struck him in the leg, passing through the muscle. We got across without difficulty, however, and two days and nights passed without a hint of shelling. Before I could become optimistic about the peace lasting, however, the bombardment recommenced with greater savagery than usual. I lay in bed listening to the noise of shells coming closer and closer until I realised that once again it was time to take the eiderdown and go and lie down in the corridor. No sooner had I collected Tara and Sasha than a shell burst very close by indeed, and I heard the sound of breaking glass from the bedroom – one of the windows had been shattered, as I discovered four hours later, when I plucked up the courage to go and look. For the umpteenth time, I wondered if I wasn't being a fool to keep risking my life, or, possibly worse, the loss of an arm or leg, by staying on in Beirut on the slim chance of Jackie's release.

At last the dawn broke. All was quiet, and the sun shone brightly into the flat. I made some tea, and decided that I'd take Tara out for a walk there and then to see what damage had been done. The wreckage was considerable, and God alone knows how Jaroudy Buildings escaped being hit.

On my return home, I found a BBC television crew waiting at the door for another interview. I was asked if I thought Jackie might now be released quite quickly, owing to the intervention of Algeria in the hostage crisis. I simply said that I didn't want to raise my hopes too quickly, as I had gone through a false dawn before and been disappointed; but of course I was praying that this time it would really happen. I was right not to be too hopeful. When I switched on the news in English in the evening there was an announcement to the effect that the Hezbollah would not now consider an exchange of prisoners. We were back to square one again.

I did not have much time to brood, for there was a telephone call from Brent to ask me to return to Jounieh with Mehdi the next day, as he wanted to do a live interview with me to be sent to England via a satellite link. This was very exciting news, and cheered me up immensely, so I packed my little suitcase again, cleaned up Tara, and went back to the Montemar with Mehdi.

We did the interview a couple of miles from Jounieh, up the mountains in the grounds of a beautiful villa. I was very nervous, as this was the first live interview I'd done; but Brent and his young cameraman, Sam, were a great help, impressing on me that I had to keep very still, and wait for the 'thumbs up' signal to start talking. By the second of the two scheduled transmissions I felt much more relaxed. As usual, I hoped that my television appearances would remind people of Jackie's fate, and perhaps persuade the British government to do something to help him and his fellow hostages.

Once home again, the shelling forced me to spend another night 'on the concrete', which is not conducive to sleep, and for the first time in my experience they were still at it the following morning as late as 8.30, which meant that I could not take Tara out. It was particularly tough in midsummer for all of us in West Beirut. The airport was still closed, the crossing point to the East Side was risky, and unless one had considerable money or influence one was effectively trapped. I try not to think too much about Jackie, reminding myself of Amine's advice, that brooding won't help him, and will only do me harm. But I cannot stave off other thoughts – like, how long it will be before my luck runs out, and the shell with my name on it falls, and I go the way of thousands of other civilians who have died for no reason down the years.

The thoughts of all of us in West Beirut swung like a pendulum between hope and anxiety. By August, we were all wondering, with our usual scepticism, what the UN might achieve in the way of a ceasefire. On the 17th, General Aoun agreed in principle, on condition that the blockade on the East was lifted. Syria was more non-committal, but agreed to try to control the militias. In the meantime, we had gone six days with no electricity at all. I had no water, and no woman friend to talk to, as Kay Daouk and Susan Barajny had both left for England until the situation eased. The heat was killing, and my morale was at an all-time low. I would sit for hours on the balcony when it was safe to do so, trying to catch a little sea-breeze, and discussing with Tara the pros and cons of what we were to do with our lives. Looking back on that period now, I doubt if I was quite normal.

Rescue came in the shape of Robert Fisk, who writes for the *Independent*, and lives in West Beirut, in a flat in Manara. He had just returned from England and had brought several letters for me back with him. This was very cheering news, as I had not had any post through normal channels for six months and more, due to the closure of the airport. I met Robert in a small bar off Sadat Street which is frequently used by foreign correspondents. Some of the letters he had brought were from the unknown well-wishers whom I have already mentioned, and contained gifts of money for 'day-to-day expenses'. I was very touched by their kindness, and their hopes for Jackie's early release, and I went home in a much more cheerful frame of mind.

At the riding club, although few people were using it, all

was well. None of the horses had been injured, though seven or eight shells had fallen in the ring, and two in the garden of the clubhouse. The worst thing was that we were not making ends meet, and Amine once again was faced with the difficult decision whether or not to close down. But if we did, who would we sell to, to cover our debts? No one would buy a riding club as things stand at the moment. Amine had another problem. His new Mazda had been stolen. His chauffeur was parked in Raouche when another car pulled up alongside him and three armed men got out. Ahmed started the engine immediately, but they shot him in the shoulder, threw him out of the car, and drove it away. This is the second car that Amine has had stolen inside a year. It makes me nervous to think that such actions may mean that the Syrians are losing their control of the militias in West Beirut. That could mean a resurgence of kidnaps, car-bombs, hold-ups and street fighting. My anxiety was increased by the fact that at the time I hadn't seen Mehdi for over ten days, and I was beginning to get worried about him, knowing his habit of always being in the thick of the fighting, taking his everlasting photographs.

Once again I was pleasantly distracted by going for drinks with Robert Fisk and his fiancée, who is also a journalist. Their balcony has a lovely view over the sea, and when I was there it was quiet, and the sea sparkled in the sunshine. Robert told me that it was a different story at night, however, as shells from East Beirut fell within yards of their apartment block. I had noticed some of the bomb craters myself, and wondered how the two of them had the courage to stay in Manara, where the shelling is especially fierce. The answer was simple; they loved their home, and were determined that no bombardment from East Beirut would move them. We all feel the same; partition of Beirut has made us all very proud of our own districts.

The August heat was now at its worst, and with no fans or air-conditioning life was intolerable. Through Amine, I managed to make an appointment to see the much respected Muslim Prime Minister, Selim Hoss, in the hope that he might

be able to exert influence to help Jackie. With every day that
passed I grew more depressed; why was there no news of him
at all? On the World Service of the BBC, I heard that rain had
stopped the cricket in England. I imagined how blissful it would
be to stand on the deserted pitch without an umbrella, and feel
the lovely rain soak into me.

I had to keep going somehow, and my lifeline was the club.
I took some carrots for the horses down there recently, as well
as some food for the colony of cats which has established itself
in our precincts. On my way home, some sporadic shelling
started, so instead of driving back my usual way, I went through
the refugee village nearby to avoid being an isolated target on
the open road. As I was approaching the end of the narrow,
winding main street with its little brick and plaster houses, a
car suddenly came out of a side turning and pulled in front
of me, blocking the road. I had a sharp stab of fear, as there
was no way to turn my car to get away. Three bearded men
climbed out of the other car and came towards me. I left the
window open for Tara to bark at them. She is a most friendly
and sweet poodle in the normal way, but once she is in the car,
she becomes a completely different animal; no one she dislikes
is going to get into *her* car.

I waited to see what the men would say, ready to give them
the car if they would only let me and Tara go free. But I was so
afraid that I couldn't speak. They talked to me in Arabic, which
I could understand, though I pretended not to. Meanwhile, Tara
continued to scream abuse from her open window. I shook my
head dimly at everything they said, and it became clear to me
that they thought I was deaf. I played along with this, realising
that it was my only hope of escape. The Muslims are deeply
religious people, and anyone who is afflicted must, according
to the Koran, be gently treated. I questioned Tara, smiled,
and offered them my purse, which had about four thousand
Lebanese pounds in it, which I could ill afford to lose; but
anything was better than being taken captive. I smiled again,
and suddenly I was free. They got back into their car, reversed

it out of the way, and allowed me to pass. The shells were still falling, but by that time I couldn't have cared less about them.

I had had a lucky escape, but my elation had turned sour by the time I got home. I knew that I was living on borrowed time; how much longer would I stay lucky?

For a few nights I managed not to leave my bed, but on 26 August all hell was let loose. A ship with a cargo of petrol was trying to get into Jounieh under cover of darkness, but the Syrians were ready for her. A terrific barrage started up, and they scored a direct hit, killing nine of the crew. At once General Aoun retaliated. I fled to the corridor and spent the rest of the night as usual in total darkness, only illuminated by the flash of explosions. In the bleak morning as I looked at my haggard reflection in the mirror, I wondered if Jackie, too, had survived this terrible night.

Worse was to come. On the night of the 31st, no less than seventeen large rockets passed over the flat, between 7.30 pm and 3 am the following morning. Each one approached with a terrifying hiss, and each time I braced myself for the impact as it hit our building. Every time they found other marks, exploding only a few hundred yards away. All of us were in a complete state of terror. Tara was shaking like a leaf, and Sasha, who had recently taken to lying down with us during raids, or hiding in a cubby-hole Jackie had long ago specially prepared for her, now once again ran around the flat like a maniac. It was a nightmare. We listened to the hiss of the rockets, the hammering of the explosions, and the wail of the ambulance sirens. I lay on the floor with Tara and cried quietly, as once more I reviewed my life in Beirut.

Eventually, at about 4.45 am, everything died down. It was impossible to try to sleep. My nerves were stretched to breaking point. I went into the kitchen and made some tea, but my thoughts were still dismal. I wondered if this last raid had not also been the last straw for me. I had had enough. In the flat I had a bottle of Gardenol tablets, kept in case a horse should ever have to be put down in an emergency, before a vet could be called. I emptied the tablets on to the kitchen table, calculating how many would be needed. If I did not take Sasha and Tara with me, there would be enough; but I could not leave them alone. By the grace of God, the telephone rang, and it was Brent, to see how I was. He talked to me for an hour, until he was sure that I was all right. That saved me.

Everything ends some time, and so did that night. The sun came up and the sea sparkled. Sasha stretched, and returned to normal. I took Tara for her morning walk. The damage was appalling. The road was pitted with large craters and strewn with broken glass. Several cars were still smouldering where they had been hit, and in the distance the smoke from several fires could be seen.

I had had some news which might have been connected with Jackie, shortly after his disappearance. At that time, an approach was made to the British Embassy, through one of their go-betweens, by people purporting to be the kidnappers, asking for medicine, but only requesting some general painkillers. They might have been for any hostage. There was no specific medicine mentioned that I might have been able to connect with Jackie. Then, on 4 September, I had another telephone call. Once again, an unidentified male voice asked if I were Mrs Mann. I told him that I was, and he said that he had some information about Jackie. Would I meet him at the riding club?

'What is it you want to tell me?'

'I'd rather not tell you over the telephone. Please.'

It was a Monday, the day when the club is normally closed for the horses and grooms to have time off, and I was immediately suspicious. The club would be deserted, and I was not going to be lured out there by a would-be kidnapper. I told him I'd meet him, but not at the riding club. He didn't insist, but suggested instead an address in Hamra Street.

'We could meet there at eleven o'clock. Please. It is very important.'

That certainly sounded safer. Hamra is in the shopping district, and there would be plenty of people around at eleven o'clock. I agreed, and shortly before eleven, drove down there.

The address proved to be that of a small shop which must once have been a jeweller's, though now its velvet-covered shelves were empty. I went in, still rather nervous, and found a man waiting for me. He was in his late forties, with grey hair, casually but very elegantly dressed, and he spoke impeccable English.

'Hello. You are Mrs Mann?'

'Yes.'

'I am glad that you have come, but I am afraid that the news I have is very bad.'

'What is it?'

'We have to tell you that your husband is dead.'

He said it as simply as that. The shock was enormous, as I hadn't been expecting it – a ransom demand perhaps, some final contact, but not that. I was shattered.

'How do you know?'

'We cannot tell you that; it might be too dangerous for you to know.' He seemed very nervous himself.

He then offered me a chair by the counter to sit on, and asked me if I'd like some coffee. I said yes, and he went immediately behind a curtained partition to make it. Even in my state, two things struck me: he had said 'we', not 'I' – and his English was too good for that to have just been a mistake. He was also clearly familiar enough with this shop to know where the coffee was.

I drank the coffee, and then, bizarrely, he gave me his name, in case I wanted to contact him again; but he swore me to secrecy – 'for both our sakes.'

After I had recovered somewhat, he even offered to drive me home, as he could see what kind of state I was in. I refused, though he insisted, gently: 'Obviously you have had a terrible shock . . .'. I knew, however, that Rule One was not to get into a car with a stranger – you could be driven anywhere.

'My car's outside and I'm all right to drive,' I said. Again, he did not press me. Slightly emboldened by his attitude, I asked him – remembering his use of the first person plural – whom he represented. Again, most surprisingly, he agreed to tell me – but with the condition that I never disclose the name, on pain of death.

As the interview was now over, I drove home and promptly collapsed into a chair. Tara jumped on to my knee. I thought about what had happened all day, and in the evening I rang Amine. He was, as always, a tower of strength. He promised to make one or two discreet enquiries, and to come and see me the following evening. Sleep was out of the question, but by the morning, having spent all night worrying at the news I'd heard, I had come to the conclusion that it wasn't true. I was sure I would have felt something if Jackie was really dead. The question that bothered me was whether or not I should tell my story to the press – without of course mentioning any names. If I could have got hold of Mehdi he might have put me in touch with Brent, who would have told me what to do for the best; but Mehdi had just been released from hospital, and was recuperating somewhere in the mountains from the wound he had received from a piece of shrapnel which had lodged in his upper left arm while he was filming in the south. I had to make my decision on my own.

After two days, I came to the conclusion that I should speak to the newspapers. Amine agreed with me. I hadn't told him the names I'd been given, nor did he ask for them. Everyone knows me, and knows my routine. Anyone could kill me at any time they chose. But at least if the story was made public, that might flush out the truth of the matter – whether Jackie was really dead or not. It meant braving the rigours of a press conference again, and no sooner had the story broken than I was besieged by yelling and screaming reporters in my flat once again – *Give us the names!* they would shout. And: *How do you feel?*

Not long after this, on 9 September, I had a visit from an

extremely unpleasant Syrian intelligence officer, the main thrust of whose questions was why hadn't I noticed the colour of the eyes of the man in the shop, and other idiocies. I told him that I had been too shocked to start picking up little details, however important. He did not appear to understand this, and I told him that the interview was at an end. I suppose I behaved badly, and said all the wrong things, but his complete disregard of how I might be feeling about my husband's possible death made me very angry.

Once again I shrank into the world of my own thoughts, though outwardly I continued to shop, clean, ride, walk Tara, and so on. But in my mind I would be dancing with Jackie at the Dorchester, and the orchestra would be playing 'Yours'.

I was brought out of this by a telephone call from the British Embassy. The Vice-Consul wanted me to cross to the East Side to talk to her about the incident; but because there was heavy shelling around the crossing at that time, I refused to go. Instead, I was asked to go down to the British Consul's office in West Beirut, to talk to her on a special private line from there. The telephone looked more like a walkie-talkie, which you had to switch on and say 'Over' into. The Vice-Consul assured me that it was an absolutely safe line, which could not possibly be tapped into. I told her the whole story, but still baulked at giving the name of the contact. She then asked me if at least I would give her the initials, so that she could check them against the list of known go-betweens. I refused to do that, but suggested that if she read out her list to me, giving the initials only, I would say 'yes' or 'no' to them. She read out a list of eight, but none concurred with those of Mr X, as I called the man whose name the go-between in the jeweller's shop had given me. Finally I said that if I had to go to Cyprus again, as I expected to at the time in order to do some more work on this book, I would release the names to the Embassy there, which could then relay it. And so it was left.

A little after this, I made contact with Mr X myself, as I was unable to leave the matter unresolved. From his name, I was able to trace who he was and where he worked. He had a Christian first name, that I can say, and he worked with Lloyd's insurance company. I wanted his private number, but he was ex-directory. Using the idea of reinsuring some of our more valuable horses, now that the fighting seemed to be in abeyance, as an excuse, I had a friend in MEA's offices dig out the ex-directory number for me.

I telephoned, and Mr X himself answered.

'You don't know me personally,' I said, 'but you may have heard of me, as I help run a riding school and we used to insure our horses with Lloyd's before the troubles. The director and myself have now decided to reinsure one or two of the better horses. I wonder if we could meet to discuss this?'

He said he would be delighted. He didn't question how I'd got his number. I was shaking in my shoes. He suggested that I ring again the following day. Having established that he was there, I decided not to telephone from my flat, as the line is tapped by the Syrians, so I went over to a friend's flat – someone who has a safe line – and I phoned from there. Then, when I got through to him, I confronted him with the real reason for getting in touch: 'Where and how did you get news of my husband's death?'

The man changed completely from being an ordinary, amiable business man to a hysteric. 'Who told you that I knew anything about your husband?' he yelled. 'If anyone told you that I'd read it in a newspaper, they're lying!' I hadn't mentioned any newspaper, nor had anyone said anything to me about an article. The man ranted on: 'I'm going to the East Side tomorrow for good,' he said. 'And then I hope to emigrate to Canada with my family!' With that, he slammed the phone down on me.

The whole business was very odd, very circumstantial. After that, I finally gave Amine the name, on condition that any enquiries his friends might be able to make would be conducted only on the East Side. But it seems that there was a great mystery connected with Mr X. No one could find out anything more about him, and the story still does not have a proper ending. Either he was acting sincerely from false information, or it was all a terrible hoax. And what newspaper carried the report of Jackie's death? I never heard of one. And why was the go-between in the jeweller's shop so helpful and sympathetic? I even went back to the shop once, and there he was. He was extremely nervous when he saw me again, and kept repeating that he knew no more than he had already told me. 'I'm not a contact,' he said. 'Please don't disclose my name to anyone.' There must have been something about Mr X to frighten this man so much, but none of us has been able to work out what it was. It was all like a bad spy thriller plot – and I felt a bit like Mata Hari – only, of course, about a hundred years older.

A second contact was made some time later, again through the Embassy, when a specific request was made for Lanacane cream. That was when I knew that Jackie was alive. None of the other hostages would have needed that particular cream, which is a salve for the kind of skin condition Jackie had following his burns and their treatment. A friend of ours, a fellow pilot called Cubby de Souza, got the ointment from the UK for me. Finally I had a message from the kidnappers via a personal contact that Jackie was alive, but that he was very weak. That seemed far more plausible, though scarcely less worrying, than the news that he was dead; and that, at the time of writing this, is the last news that I have had of him.

I had not been able to buy anything for myself since Jackie was kidnapped, as the little money I had was needed for food for the animals, petrol, benzine for the generator and other household expenses. If there was any left over, I would buy cheese, fruit and eggs for myself. I was eating less than ever owing to worry and the summer heat. Life feels like solitary confinement. I am afraid to venture too far from the flat for too long, and my only full-time companions are Tara and Sasha. By now Tara is starting to understand English very well, and she is a great comfort to me. Sasha too is becoming more and more affectionate. She is so scared of the shelling that she clings increasingly to me, though that tends to make Tara jealous. Tara remembers the amount of attention Sasha used to get from Jackie, and regards me as her *personal* friend. Meanwhile, we await the outcome of further peace talks, without any great hope that they will bring a permanent settlement. Syria will stay until Israel moves out, and it does not look as if Israel will budge. Meanwhile the permanently deadlocked battle of Beirut continues. Food prices rise, the poor people in the refugee camps in the southern suburbs demonstrate because they cannot afford to eat, and nothing is done because no government can function. War-injured people have appeared as beggars for the first time on the city streets. The Arab tradition of family life seems to be breaking down too. The old are no longer looked after by the young and strong.

Two contrasting experiences I have had recently. The first was an anonymous phone call in the middle of the night. Tara heard the phone ringing and aroused me with her barking. A man's voice: *Why don't you leave Beirut?* Then he hung up. This kind of thing makes me very much afraid. I do not know if I can get my number changed, go ex-directory. The chain on my door would not prevent anyone breaking it down if they wanted to.

The second event began more cheerfully. I had a telex from Brent, via Mehdi, to say that ITN were prepared to fly my daughter Jennifer and my nephew David down to Cyprus to see me and stay with me for a two-week holiday. This was wonderful news, as I hadn't seen any of my family for almost three years. My first reaction was what would I do with the animals, as I will not leave them for more than a couple of days, however well my neighbours look after them, and if they went to Cyprus there would be the problem of quarantine. But Brent had thought of that, and arranged with the authorities for both animals to go into house quarantine at the home of my kind friends Hector and Elaine. I was very excited, and started to look for travelling baskets for Tara and Sasha. At that time, Beirut airport was still closed, and I would have to fly from Damascus, a four-hour drive away. I also did my accounts to see if I could afford a new blouse for this very special occasion. I knew that we would be surrounded by newspaper and television cameramen, but I welcomed any publicity that would help Jackie.

I need not have worried. Five days later Brent rang to say that Jennifer had decided that she was not well enough to face the journey after her recent cancer operation. I did not blame her at all, as I knew very well how daunting the media can be; but I was very disappointed, as I had so looked forward to seeing both of them, after such a long time. I was getting used to disappointments, though. I saved my money, and went on wearing my old blouses.

On 17 September I had worrying news from Mahmoud, who runs the garage Jackie and I use, and who had been looking after the Simca. I had told him he could use it if he wanted to, as he was letting me store it with him free. He told me that the day before, he had been followed home by another car. He had not stopped at his house, but drove fast around side roads until he had shaken off his pursuer. He then made his way back to his garage and hid the Simca in a back corner. He was very shaken, as one of his brothers was shot and killed on the Airport Road only a year ago.

The incident seemed to be just another nail in the coffin of my nerves. It is exhausting, having to live as I do, constantly on the alert, at my age. I long to be able to unlock the door of this city and leave it; I have always loved Beirut, but it has become a prison for me, and I am not sure if I can stand it much longer. Everyone leaves as soon as they can, except for a few who have great or deep commitments. When I recently pulled a tendon in my neck I went to see a doctor recommended by a friend, as my own doctor is inaccessible, on the East Side. This man gave me some painkillers and told me not to lift anything heavier than a kilogram. I took the pills, but had to ignore the advice because there is no one else to carry my water or my shopping, and poor Mehdi has a family of his own and cannot be with me every hour of the day. When I wanted to consult the doctor again, because the pain was, unsurprisingly, not letting up, his receptionist told me he had gone to the USA. The only doctors left now are juniors; as soon as they are fully qualified, they will leave too.

On 21 September a prominent Sunni ex-minister was shot dead in the street in broad daylight. More and more it looks as if the Syrians are losing control of the militias. Fear is in the air once more, and people are not going far from their homes if they can help it. At night the streets are deserted, and Beirut is a ghost town again.

However, I still took Tara for her walks, though I always looked over my shoulder. I was still determined – still am – that no one was going to force me to leave. I was also preparing a direct appeal to President Assad of Syria, which was something of a last resort; but I can leave no stone unturned in trying to get Jackie released. One day, I had another narrow escape. I had driven down to Manara, which is not the safest district, but there is a depot there where you can buy beer wholesale, and as my budget is tight, I always get my beer there. The depot is at the end of a cul-de-sac, and I am always rather nervous while I am waiting for the man there to exchange the empty cases for full ones. The assistant had just put my two new cases in the boot of my Honda when another car pulled in behind me. I got out and walked back to ask the driver to reverse so that I could drive out. He promptly pulled a gun on me and told me that they wanted my car. There were three of them, again. For a moment I was frozen with fright and could not speak. I could see that I was not going to get any help from the workers at the depot, who had made themselves scarce, so I did the obvious female thing and burst into tears, telling them that I was the wife of the hostage, Jackie Mann, that I needed my car to get around in order to see people who might be able to help me get my husband freed.

To my astonishment, their attitude changed immediately.

They put their guns away, gathered round me sympathetically, and told me that if there was anything they could do to help, then or in the future, I had only to get in touch. I accepted the contact number they gave me, and at my suggestion we all went off for a coffee together. We parted the best of friends.

By the end of September, the peace negotiators had made enough progress for the airport to reopen. The crossings between East and West Beirut were also reopened, and more strictly controlled than they had been before. Residents began to trickle back into the city from the countryside and abroad, and there was even talk of reopening the schools.

My mood, and that of many in West Beirut, was still cautious. We had learned that 'wait and see' was the best policy. It was foolhardy to celebrate too soon. Unexpectedly, Mehdi appeared after an absence of over a week, and I was rather cross with him, just because my nerves are in a permanently ragged state. Poor Mehdi was very upset. Before he left, he told me he would like to buy me two new pairs of slacks as a present to make friends again. It is kind of him. All my clothes are falling to pieces.

The atmosphere of careful optimism was dashed for me by a personal tragedy. A young man who had learned to ride with me, and whom I had known since the age of twelve, committed suicide with his young wife. They could not stand the tension of life in Beirut any more. They had been found locked in each other's arms in a gas-filled bathroom at his father's house. They had been married for six years, and were very much in love. I felt like following them, and went about for four days in a state of the blackest despair. But once again a phone call from Brent saved me. He wanted me to go over to the East Side to discuss plans for this book – it seemed that a publisher in England was interested, and a contract was in the offing. I was happy to see him again, and we had champagne at dinner to celebrate. As Julie Flint had not been able to return from England, Brent also recorded my appeal to President Assad, so that it would be available for transmission when the time was most propitious.

And so I continue. I take great pleasure in teaching my star young pupil, six-year-old Karim Abbas, to ride on Bijou II. I continue to manage the day-to-day struggle with shopping, washing, walking Tara. It seems inconceivable to me that elsewhere these are simple, even pleasurable tasks, not burdensome labours. Despite further talks, and peace agreements which have come close to taking hold, the situation here is still volatile. On 22 November the new president, Rene Moawad, whose authority was denied by General Aoun, was killed by a car-bomb after only seventeen days in office. The shells still fly over, I still accept that there will be nights spent sleeping on the floor of the corridor in the flat. Like my own story, Lebanon's has yet to have an ending. We wait sadly together for some kind of happiness to return. People ask me to be patient. I try to be.

As I was writing this book, I used to sit on the balcony of my flat, surrounded by the shattered buildings of Raouche. I would look at the sun setting over the sea and think about what the future held. Tara would be on my lap, and I used to tell her everything that I wrote down, and ask her if it was to her liking. For answer, she might just move a paw, to show that she was not quite comfortable, and I would have to press my legs closer together to provide a better platform, arching my arm around her to reach the table to write.

'Better now?' I would say. 'Can I go on?' And she would wag her tail. But after a few moments she would move again, and I would say, 'Yes, I know, Tara, I haven't mentioned the big crater that was left down by the Pigeon Rocks the day the car-bomb went off there. But now I've put it in. Good enough?' She was like having a child around: a bit irritating, but indispensable when you are trying to write, with her interruptions: what about this? Have you forgotten that? Why don't you put that in? I cannot describe it other than to say that she was human to me. I loved her so much. She was really all that I had.

Two days before Christmas 1989, Tara and I were returning

from our usual walk when a man pushed me to the ground and grabbed her. He ran off. I have not seen her since, and I will never see her again. But I will not leave.

It is evening now, and growing too dark for me to write any more. In any case I have come to the end of my story – as far as I can tell it. Be with me again soon, Jackie. I love you, darling. May Allah protect you.

The sun is touching the sea. In a moment I will go in, and maybe have a beer. At least it will be cold; the generator is working at the moment, and there hasn't been any shelling.

Perhaps tomorrow there will be news.